INSPIRING VOICES

15 Interviews from NHK Direct Talk

Megumi Kobayashi
Reiko Fujita
Peter J. Collins

KINSEIDO

Kinseido Publishing Co., Ltd.

3-21 Kanda Jimbo-cho, Chiyoda-ku,
Tokyo 101-0051, Japan

Copyright © 2021 by Megumi Kobayashi
Reiko Fujita
Peter J. Collins

First published 2021 by Kinseido Publishing Co., Ltd.

Design: Nampoosha Co., Ltd:

Video materials: NHK (Japan Broadcasting Corporation)

The authors and publisher are grateful to NHK Global Media Services, Inc.,
National Institute of Polar Research (Voice 6, pp. 41- 46),
and all the interviewees who appeared in the interviews.
The authors would like to thank Ms. Aoi Nishida of Kinseido Publishing
for her initiative and constant support throughout this project.

🎧 音声ファイル無料ダウンロード

https://www.kinsei-do.co.jp/download/4120

この教科書で 🎧 DL 00 の表示がある箇所の音声は、上記 URL または QR コードにて
無料でダウンロードできます。自習用音声としてご活用ください。

- ▶ PC からのダウンロードをお勧めします。スマートフォンなどでダウンロードされる場合は、
  ダウンロード前に「**解凍アプリ**」をインストールしてください。
- ▶ URL は、**検索ボックスではなくアドレスバー（URL 表示欄）** に入力してください。
- ▶ お使いのネットワーク環境によっては、ダウンロードできない場合があります。

◎ **CD 00** 左記の表示がある箇所の音声は、教室用 CD（Class Audio CD）に収録されています。

Welcome to *Inspiring Voices*

Every day, we use our voices to meet all kinds of communication goals. We might need to share a secret or ask for help. Maybe we want to tell a joke or to change someone's mind. Or our goal may be to **inspire** others to think differently and to take action. Succeeding in all these goals requires effectively communicating what we know, what we believe, and what we wish for. This can be a challenge, and doing it in a second language can be even more so.

The goal of *Inspiring Voices* is to help you build the skills you need to meet this challenge. Each of the 15 chapters features an NHK *Direct Talk* interview with a creative problem-solver. Whether they are working with women in a Japanese fishing village or developing new ways to explore outer space, each interviewee has a dream for, a plan for, and a message about making the world a better place.

The activities in each chapter are sequenced to support your understanding of each interview and to give you plenty of chances to advance all four English skills. There is also a balance of individual work, pair work, and group work that will help you participate meaningfully in class. The activities' emphasis on target language in context will give you the language you need to both understand and react to each interview. Thinking skills are important too; you'll develop them by identifying and organizing key information into tables and charts.

At the end of every chapter, you'll be invited to collaborate with a small group of your classmates to complete a mini-project. This is an extra opportunity to reflect on what you have learned and to apply it as you imagine yourselves as teachers, business owners, and even scientists.

It's easy to imagine that, as each interviewee has worked to change the lives of the people around them, they have noticed positive changes in their own lives as well. Hopefully, their stories will inspire your own voice!

Using *Inspiring Voices*

The activity sequence in each chapter will help you build the kinds of knowledge, language, and communication skills you need to succeed in today's global society.

Sharing Our Views

After you read the chapter preview, you'll see three discussion questions related to the interview topic. They'll give you and your partner or group a chance to start thinking about the interview topic as you share your own experiences and opinions.

Building Background

This passage will help prepare you to watch the interview. Reading the passage and answering True/False questions will familiarize you with both the topic and some core vocabulary of the interview.

Boosting Vocabulary

This is your chance to confirm the definitions of more vocabulary that will come up in the interview.

Introduction — Understanding the Main Topic

1st Listening

As you watch the introductory part by a news anchor in Part 1 of the interview, you'll confirm basic facts about the person being interviewed by checking the correct statements. Note that the audio version is narrated at a slower speed than the video.

2nd Listening

As you watch again, you'll focus on important details as you complete the script by filling in the blanks.

Interview

(online / video)

Checking Key Points

Part 1 of the interview is 4-5 minutes. As you watch it, you'll confirm key facts by choosing the option that best completes each sentence.

Organizing Information

After watching Part 1 again, you'll organize the key information by completing a table, chart, or summary.

Interview

(online / video)

Checking Key Points

Part 2 is also 4-5 minutes. As you watch it, you'll confirm key facts by choosing the option that best completes each sentence.

Organizing Information

After watching Part 2 again, you'll organize the key information by completing a table, chart, or summary.

The Words to Live By

(online / video) (online / audio)

Here you'll focus on the meaning of the interviewee's core message as you complete the script by filling in the blanks. Again, the audio version is narrated at a slower speed than the video.

Sharing Our Responses

This is your chance to reflect on and react, in your own words, to the interview. In **1**, you'll write down three things you learned. In **2**, you'll write short messages to people mentioned in the interview. If time allows, you can share what you've written with a partner or a group.

Taking the Next Step

Here is your opportunity to work with a group on a mini-project! Together, you'll apply what you've learned by brainstorming ways to tackle an issue. If time allows, your group can share your ideas with the class. Can you persuade them that your idea can solve the problem?

INSPIRING VOICES

15 Interviews from NHK Direct Talk

Contents

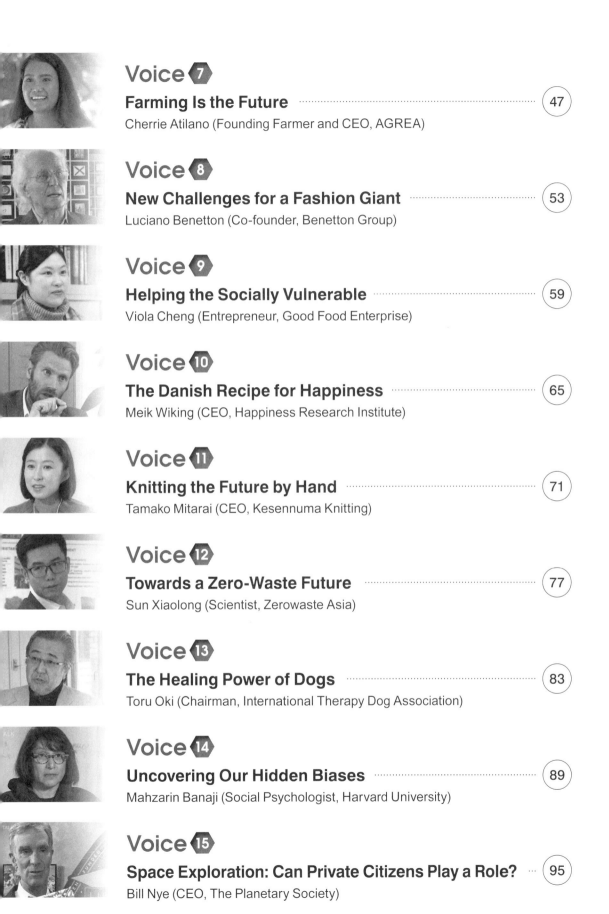

Nadiem Makarim

Ride-Hailing Innovation: Creating Jobs Through Technology

In this chapter, we'll take a look at a venture company in Indonesia, where economic growth has recently been very rapid. Let's learn about a young entrepreneur's attempt to create jobs through technology.

Sharing Our Views

Think about the following questions and talk with your partner.

1. When, where, and how often do you use taxis? Do you think they are convenient?

2. When you use a taxi, what is the most important factor for you: speed, comfort, price, or safety?

3. What smartphone applications make your daily life more convenient? What did you do before you started using them?

Read the latest post by a popular travel blogger and answer the True/False questions below. The words in bold will appear in the interview.

Ojeks: Couldn't live without them!

After two weeks of traveling around Indonesia, I'm back in Jakarta, the country's **bustling** capital. Shopping in the Menteng Flea Market, visiting Ragunan Zoo, spending the day on Ancol Beach... And my favorite way to get from one place to another? *Ojeks!* An *ojek* is a privately-owned motorcycle taxi, and there are **literally** thousands of them in Jakarta. You can find them parked and ready all over the city. I've been taking them on a daily basis, both here and

By Sheri Steinberg
Updated 18 March
Posted in Jakarta

in rural areas, and I have to admit—I'm really crazy about *ojeks*! But I've also learned some important lessons about taking them.

For one thing, if you approach a driver on the street, don't jump onto the back of his *ojek* until you've reached a mutual agreement on the price. And if you sense that he's not a **conscientious**, safe driver, don't be shy about asking him to let you get off.

For another thing, a more **reliable** option is to use a **ride-hailing** app like Gojek; it's similar to an app you would use to book a regular taxi. You enter your location and your destination and an *ojek* is **dispatched** right away. And because of the meter, there's never a disagreement about the fare. The success of ride-hailing apps has **given rise to** new kinds of *ojek* apps, for example delivery services. My driver yesterday told me that these apps have had a big **impact** on his workday.

Off to see the National Museum—you'll read about it in my next post!

1. *Ojeks* are not generally available in the rural areas of Indonesia. T / F

2. Sheri advises deciding on the fare before taking an *ojek* anywhere. T / F

3. Apps like Gojek allow drivers to set their own fares and destinations. T / F

Boosting Vocabulary

online audio   DL 03   CD 03

Match these words from the interview with their definitions.

1. perception   _____   **a.** strong, unlikely to fail
2. stabilize   _____   **b.** stop changing
3. robust   _____   **c.** think about something all the time
4. ineligible   _____   **d.** impression, opinion
5. capital   _____   **e.** not allowed to participate
6. worthwhile   _____   **f.** deserving of time and effort
7. obsess   _____   **g.** money, assets

Introduction   Understanding the Main Topic   ▶ Part 1 0:00–0:56

online video   online audio   DL 04   CD 04

 **1st Listening**   Check ☑ the correct statements.

Nadiem Makarim _____.

- ☐ is a motorcycle manufacturer
- ☐ started a venture business
- ☐ invented two-wheeled taxis
- ☐ has created more employment

 **2nd Listening**   Complete the script by filling in the blanks.

Welcome to *Direct Talk*. Today's guest: Gojek CEO Nadiem Makarim. In Indonesia, a nation of 260 million that's seen [1]( ) economic growth in recent years, he's taking the world by storm with a smartphone app [2]( ). In the cities of Southeast Asia, [3]( ) has been unable to keep up with growth, making two-wheeled taxis a familiar way to get around. The smartphone app [4]( ) motorcycle taxis. It can also be used to order food delivery or get a massage. This convenience has resulted in over 100 million [5]( ). It's also created new jobs. Now at the height of the IT [6]( ), we spoke with Nadiem Makarim on how technology can lead to social change.

Checking Key Points

Watch Part 1 and choose the correct answers.

1. An *ojek* is a form of transportation that can be offered by anyone who owns a (car / motorcycle).

2. On average, many *ojek* drivers Makarim met were getting (three / twelve) customers a day.

3. Makarim noticed that there was an (imbalance / equilibrium) in *ojek* supply and demand.

4. When Makarim started his business, twenty drivers (applied / were hand-picked) for jobs with the company.

5. Gojek first started as (a call center / an online service provider).

Organizing Information

Compare life before and after Gojek by completing the table. The first letters are provided.

	Before: *ojek*	After: Gojek
Drivers	Anyone	Those [1](r) with the company
System	Waiting around for hours	Easily [2](h) through an app
Rates	Occasional overcharge	[3](R) prices
Image	Untrustworthy, unhygienic	Trustworthy, clean image, wearing green company [4](j)
Safety	Not following rules	Conscientious
Service	Transport people	Transport both people and [5](g)
Income	Unstable	[6](S)

Interview [4:34]

online video

Checking Key Points

Watch Part 2 and choose the correct answers.

1. One problem was that people were looking for jobs (without having social security / within the welfare system).

2. Makarim firmly believes that technology can (take people's jobs away / give people opportunities).

3. Traditionally, many women in Indonesia (continue working outside the home / quit work for a range of reasons).

4. Many successful entrepreneurs working for GoFood are (talented women / working in malls).

5. Makarim's business has now expanded (worldwide / to other Asian countries).

Organizing Information

Explain how Gojek is solving problems by completing the table with items from the box below. Some of them are extra.

Problem ①	Problem ②
Many people are outside the social system. They do not pay income tax, so are [1]( ) for social security.	Women who want to [2]( ) their careers need to stop working for reasons such as childcare.
Solution: Smartphone app technology	
Anyone with a smartphone can access the outside world with one [3]( ) and find a way to [4]( ) the market.	
Outcome ①	Outcome ②
Gojek drivers now have a reliable source of [5]( ).	GoFood offers women opportunities to continue working and [6]( ) money.

income / tap / worthwhile / pursue / earn / capture / ineligible / asset online/video   online/audio   🎧 DL 05   ⊙ CD 05

Confirm the conclusion of the interview by completing the script below.

Makarim: This is the first company value and most important company value in Gojek. It's called, "It's not about you." And

¹ _____

_____ and keeping people who are, for the large part, done with themselves and don't obsess about themselves but obsess about the problems out there in the real world. Building an organization of ² _____

_____ that's not all about them is, I think, the only way to build truly great products. And ³ _____

_____ through technology.

Sharing Our Responses

1. Write down three new facts you learned from the interview. Share them with your partner.
2. With your partner, discuss and decide on a message for each of the following: Nadiem Makarim, Gojek drivers, and women considering working for GoFood. Share your messages with your classmates.

Taking the Next Step

Your group is starting a new ride-hailing company in Japan. As a group, think about how you want to promote your company. Look up Gojek or a similar service in Japan or elsewhere for reference. Imagine the top page of a website for your company. Include:

1. The name of your company and the logo
2. The services you provide that regular taxis do not
3. The drivers and the target customers

Present your company to your classmates. Can you persuade them that your company is the best one?

Eri Machii

Bringing Medicine to the African Backcountry

In this chapter, we'll look at how a traditional Japanese method of selling medicines is being applied in Africa. Let's learn how Eri Machii, who introduced this business model there, became interested in helping people in African countries.

Sharing Our Views

Think about the following questions and talk with your partner.

1. What do you think are the most common kinds of medicine people have at home?

2. What was the longest time you ever had to wait to see a doctor? How did you feel about waiting?

3. How do you get information about medical treatments when you are sick?

Read this excerpt from a letter to volunteers joining the Better Globe Program and answer the True/False questions below. The words in bold will appear in the interview.

Staying Healthy as a Better Globe Volunteer

What kinds of health conditions will you meet in your host country? To put it simply, every situation is different. Soon, you'll receive a packet with information specific to the country where you'll be working. In the meantime, here is some general advice.

— **What to pack**

Your packet will include a country-specific list of required and recommended things to bring with you; items on the list are difficult to **procure** from **vendors** in your host country. When you arrive, you'll receive a medical kit containing basic equipment such as **bandages**, **ointments, painkillers**, and vitamins. However, you should bring at least six months of any prescription medicines with you; show the attached request form to your doctor(s).

— **What to expect**

During your six-week in-country training, you'll receive any necessary vaccines. Still, after you are **dispatched** to your individual site, you may be exposed to **infectious** diseases, **parasites**, or have other health issues. Our organization hires medical staff in each host country who work only with trusted **pharmacists**. While in your host country, you are not required to belong to an **insurance** plan; all health care **fees** are automatically covered by our organization.

Your health—and your **peace of mind**—are important to us. Please don't hesitate to contact us with any questions or concerns you have.

1. Health concerns may be different in each country volunteers work in.   T / F

2. It is best to bring enough prescription medicines to last at least half a year.
     T / F

3. Better Globe volunteers are responsible for arranging their own insurance before departing.   T / F

Boosting Vocabulary

online audio   🎧 DL 07   ⊙ CD 07

Match these words from the interview with their definitions.

1. span	_____	**a.** give information to, instruct
2. restock	_____	**b.** carry out
3. implement	_____	**c.** convenient, easy to access
4. at your fingertips	_____	**d.** basic systems and services needed by a community
5. enlighten	_____	**e.** period of time
6. infrastructure	_____	**f.** make something less harmful
7. mitigate	_____	**g.** replace goods that have been sold or used

Introduction   Understanding the Main Topic   ▶ Part 1 0:00-0:48

online video   online audio   🎧 DL 08   ⊙ CD 08

 **Check ☑ the correct statements.**

Eri Machii _____.

☐ is a doctor working in Africa

☐ runs an organization called AfriMedico

☐ is the head of a 300-year-old Japanese company

☐ provides medicine to people in Africa who need it

 **Complete the script by filling in the blanks.**

Welcome to *Direct Talk*—interviews with leaders, visionaries, and pioneers who are shaping Asia and the rest of the world. Our guest today is Eri Machii, ¹( ) and chairperson of the non-profit organization AfriMedico. Machii has introduced a more than ²( )-year-old Japanese system of selling ³( ) into Africa. She uses that system to ⁴( ) much-needed drugs to the deepest reaches of the ⁵( ) where access to health care is limited. We asked Machii about what ⁶( ) her to start up the current efforts in Africa.

Checking Key Points

Watch Part 1 and choose the correct answers.

1. *Oki-gusuri* was developed over 300 years ago in (Edo / Toyama), Japan.

2. In the *oki-gusuri* system, vendors receive payment (before / after) the medicine is used.

3. The advantage of *oki-gusuri* is that people have (immediate access to / all kinds of) medicines.

4. Machii has placed medicine boxes in 100 (households / hospitals) in Tanzania.

5. The items in the *oki-gusuri* are (imported from Japan / obtained locally).

Organizing Information

Describe the *oki-gusuri* cycle by completing the flowchart.

Vendors leave a box full of medicines at each
1 _____ .

Vendors
5 _____
the medicine box.

The family
2 _____
as needed.

People do not have to
3 _____
to get the medicine they need.

Vendors come back and
4 _____
for whatever medicine the family has used.

Interview [5:10]

online video

Checking Key Points

Watch Part 2 and choose the correct answers.

1. Machii was dispatched to (Niger / Tanzania) as a volunteer worker.

2. The majority of the villagers believed that (mosquitoes / God) caused malaria.

3. Machii tried to raise awareness of malaria's causes among the villagers by (distributing pamphlets / story-telling).

4. According to Machii, *oki-gusuri* in Japan developed partly due to the lack of (social networks / infrastructure).

5. *Oki-gusuri* payment is done by mobile devices to reduce the (risk of robbery / number of rounds staff must make).

Organizing Information

Review Machii's career by arranging the following statements in the correct order.

Eri Machii...	
1	went to India as a pharmaceutical science major.
2	
3	left her pharmaceutical job when she was 27.
4	
5	
6	
7	started an NPO.
8	

a. started introducing *oki-gusuri* in Tanazania.
b. worked to stop the spread of malaria in Niger.
c. went to Niger with a government-run program.
d. enrolled in a business school after returning to Japan.
e. volunteered to help at a home for orphans.

    DL 09 CD 09

Confirm the conclusion of the interview by completing the script below.

Machii: "Provide first, receive compensation later." ¹ _____ and payment naturally will follow. Basically, this is the business model for *oki-gusuri*. And I feel like it applies to my experiences as well. I went to Africa wanting to do something for the people. In the end, I ² _____ . When the local people tell me that they were glad we left a certain medicine or that simply having the medicines there ³ _____ , that gives me energy. It gives me the power and motivation to do what I want to do next.

Sharing Our Responses

1. Write down three new facts you learned from the interview. Share them with your partner.
2. With your partner, discuss and decide on a message for each of the following: Eri Machii, villagers in Tanzania, and future international volunteers. Share your messages with your classmates.

Taking the Next Step

As a group of volunteers, decide on a project you would like to join. Do an online search on "international volunteer opportunities" for reference. In your group, prepare a brief presentation including:

1. What country you would like to volunteer in and why
2. What kind of work you would like to do and why
3. What kind of outcomes you hope your work will have

Can you persuade your classmates to join you in your volunteer work?

Margaret Martin

Saving Children in Poverty Through Music

In this chapter, we'll learn about a teacher's project to help children in poverty through music lessons. Let's find out how music is helping these children have a better future.

Sharing Our Views

Think about the following questions and talk with your partner.

1. What musical instruments have you played? For how long?

2. Which new instrument would you like to be able to play? Why?

3. What kinds of effects do you think the experience of playing music has on people?

Building Background

Read this letter from a music teacher to parents and answer the True/False questions below. The words in bold will appear in the interview.

Dear Parents,

Another academic year is about to begin here at Milford Hills Junior High, and it's time to make decisions with your children about how best to help them **thrive** at school. As you do so, please keep our music clubs in mind: the orchestra, the marching band, and the chorus.

Why join one of these clubs? Making music provides children with a way to express themselves; it also helps them to understand their own and others' emotions. This **empathy** is vital to their emotional intelligence as they get older. Also, signing up for a music club means building friendships through shared experiences; that feeling of **inclusion** is key to children's **confidence** at this age.

And there's more good news: **comparative** studies have shown that **pursuing** an interest in music has a positive **impact** on children's sense of **discipline**; learning an instrument teaches the necessity of following routines, whether it's cleaning a flute or doing warm-up scales. Just as important is the sense of **accountability** children develop as they avoid letting down those around them. Making music also builds **persistence**; beginning musicians quickly see that improvement only comes through practice. Once a child is **hooked on** singing or playing the clarinet, they're willing to put in the work. Maybe that's why so few children **drop out** of Milford Hills' music clubs!

All skill and experience levels are welcome! Please fill out and have your child bring the attached sign-up form to their homeroom teacher by Wednesday, September 10.

Thanks,
Tracy Aitchison, Music teacher

1. The music program stresses the importance of students working independently. T / F

2. Ms. Aitchison believes that students learn responsibility through music lessons. T / F

3. Most of the students who join a music club at Milford Hills stick with it. T / F

24

Boosting Vocabulary

online/audio DL 11 CD 11

Match these words from the interview with their definitions.

1. effect _____
2. envision _____
3. intervention _____
4. juvenile _____
5. detention _____
6. enroll _____
7. mentor _____

a. action taken to improve a situation
b. not yet adult
c. imagine
d. forcing someone to stay somewhere
e. register, add one's name to a list
f. result of an influence
g. advise someone with less experience

Introduction

Understanding the Main Topic   ▶ Part 1 0:00–0:59

online/video online/audio DL 12 CD 12

1st Listening   Check ☑ the correct statements.

Harmony Project _____.
- [ ] helps children in poverty
- [ ] offers free music concerts to school children
- [ ] is a short-term training program for parents
- [ ] aims to give kids skills to succeed in society

2nd Listening   Complete the script by filling in the blanks.

Welcome to *Direct Talk*—interviews with leaders, visionaries, and pioneers who are shaping Asia and the rest of the world. Rising income inequality is leading to an increase in ¹(   ) rates around the globe, even in developed countries. Among those most ²(   ) are youths. One out of every five children in developed countries lives in poverty, according to a 2017 UNICEF report. Today, we talk to Dr. Margaret Martin, the ³(   ) of the Harmony Project. Dr. Martin believes that children from low-income families have more ⁴(   ) learning, staying in school, and developing the skills necessary to ⁵(   ) in modern society. The Harmony Project utilizes music to provide ⁶(   ) and goals to those children. Currently, more than 6,000 students receive free music lessons through the project.

Interview

Part 1 [4:40]

online / video

Checking Key Points

Watch Part 1 and choose the correct answers.

1. It is often difficult for children growing up in low-income families to (envision their future / understand what is already around them).

2. Harmony Project is open only to (teenage dropouts / children from needy families).

3. (Freelance musicians / College students) provide music instruction to the children in Harmony Project.

4. Harmony Project is a (venture company / non-profit organization).

5. Through (comparative research / interviews with graduates), it was found that children in the project were better able to control their behavior.

Organizing Information

Describe Harmony Project by completing the table. The first two blanks are numbers. The other first letters are provided.

Harmony Project	
Founder	Dr. Margaret Martin
Locations	[1]( ) sites in the U.S.
Students	Ages: [2]( ) to 18 Qualification: Children from families in [3](p) Enrollment: More than 6,000 students
Charge	[4](F)
Instructors	Musicians who are freelance
Aim	Mentor kids throughout childhood Help them develop the [5](h) of mind to lead successful lives: discipline, persistence, [6](c), accountability

Interview

Part 2

[4:48]

online video

Checking Key Points

Watch Part 2 and choose the correct answers.

1. Dr. Martin (became homeless / bought a house) when she was in her 20s.

2. Dr. Martin earned a doctorate degree in (public health / music) when she was 44.

3. More than (50 / 90)% of the first students from the project successfully graduated from high school and went on to college.

4. Playing instruments (together / independently) in Harmony Project gives students the ability to face challenges in the real world.

5. By practicing and performing music, students in the project learn to (be competitive / care about their peers).

Organizing Information

Summarize Vianney's life by completing the table with items from the box below.

Vianney...	
1	grew up in a Mexican immigrant family.
2	lived in a high-crime neighborhood in Los Angeles.
3	
4	
5	came to love the violin.
6	
7	
8	

DIRECT TALK

a. got a scholarship and studied in Mexico.
b. went to college and majored in linguistics.
c. was enrolled by her mother in Harmony Project.
d. is studying to be a certified court interpreter.
e. was sent to a juvenile detention center for fighting.

27

Part 2 3:56–4:48

online video   online audio   🎧 DL 13   ◎ CD 13

Confirm the conclusion of the interview by completing the script below.

Narrator: We asked Dr. Martin her philosophy of life.

Dr. Martin: "Never let your circumstances define you." **1** _____

_____, whether they come from a poor environment or a wealthy one. My own difficult circumstances inspired me to launch Harmony Project, which is **2**_____

_____. Everyone has difficult circumstances. Don't get stuck in them but let them inform what you do next.

3 _____.

Sharing Our Responses

1. Write down three new facts you learned from the interview. Share them with your partner.

2. With your partner, discuss and decide on a message for each of the following: Dr. Martin, Vianney, and low-income parents concerned about their children. Share your messages with your classmates.

Taking the Next Step

Income inequality and low motivation are problems at Sakura Elementary School. As a group of freelance musicians, design a music project to propose to Sakura's Board of Education. You can refer to Harmony Project's website. Include:

1. The project name and its goals
2. The target students (who, how many) and the instructors (who, how many)
3. A practice schedule and a concert calendar

Present your proposal to the class. Can you persuade them to adopt the program?

Voice

4

Takeo Sugita

The Matcha Business: A Maverick Spirit

In this chapter, we'll learn about top matcha producer Aiya. Let's find out how the company fought to get a competitive edge in the traditional Japanese tea industry by "thinking outside the box."

Sharing Our Views

Think about the following questions and talk with your partner.

1. Have you tried matcha tea? Do you like it?

2. Rank the following from 1 to 6, 1 being the most delicious flavor:
   [   ] chocolate   [   ] strawberry   [   ] matcha
   [   ] caramel   [   ] vanilla   [   ] coffee

3. Rank the following matcha-flavored products from 1 to 6, 1 being the best idea:
   [   ] cheesecake   [   ] potato chips
   [   ] chewing gum   [   ] curry
   [   ] pizza   [   ] sausages

Read this explanation and recipe from a cooking website and answer the True/ False questions below. The words in bold will appear in the interview.

Magical Matcha!

You may feel that matcha is nothing more than the latest fashion, but it's a **time-honored** beverage that was first drunk in China over a thousand years ago. In the 12th century, a Japanese monk named Eisai saw the **potential** of tea to grow into a major **enterprise** in Japan and brought seeds—and matcha-preparing techniques—back to Kyoto from China.

Most tea is in the form of dried leaves, including the **veins**, that we boil, then throw away. However, matcha is different; after it is steamed, cooled, then dried in the factory, the leaves are finely **ground** into powder we add hot water to. We **whisk** the matcha until it is **foamy** and then actually drink the powder.

When it comes to flavor, there's nothing like matcha's layers of sweetness, umami, and **astringency**. In addition, many believe that matcha is **packed with nutrients** like cancer-fighting catechins and vitamins A, B1, B6, and C. Matcha is also said to contain anti-aging and detoxifying properties, making it not only delicious but a superfood!

All my recipes here on this page include matcha, which you can buy at any supermarket these days. After you try a recipe, leave a review below it. Thanks!

Matcha Smoothie

Preparation Time: *5-10 minutes*
Calories: *150*
Ingredients: *1 cup ice cubes, 1/2 cup almond milk, 1/2 cup spinach, 1/2 cup kale, 1 small banana, 1/2 cup chopped apple, 2 tablespoons almonds, 1 teaspoon matcha powder*
Instructions: *Blend all ingredients together for 60 to 90 seconds. Makes one serving.*

1. Over 1,000 years ago, Eisai carried tea seeds to Japan from China.   T / F

2. According to the author, matcha is delicious, but not very healthy.   T / F

3. The Matcha Smoothie recipe includes vegetables, fruits, and nuts.   T / F

Boosting Vocabulary

  online audio DL 15 CD 15

Match these words from the interview with their definitions.

1. facilitate _____   **a.** grab and hold

2. rays _____   **b.** previous person holding a position

3. contend with _____   **c.** boom, trend

4. predecessor _____   **d.** independent, unconventional person

5. maverick _____   **e.** make easier, assist the progress of

6. craze _____   **f.** deal with something, confront

7. latch on to _____   **g.** sunshine

Introduction

Understanding the Main Topic   ▶ **Part 1** 0:00–0:49

online video   online audio   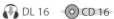 DL 16   CD 16

 **Check ☑ the correct statements.**

☐ Takeo Sugita is the president of Aiya.

☐ Aiya's operations are limited to domestic sales.

☐ Aiya makes various kinds of sweets.

☐ Sugita's family has owned Aiya for over 300 years.

 **Complete the script by filling in the blanks.**

Welcome to *Direct Talk*—interviews with leaders, visionaries, and pioneers who are shaping Asia and the rest of the world. Our guest today is Takeo Sugita, president of matcha maker Aiya. Matcha is a traditional Japanese ¹(   ). It's a type of green tea made by mixing powdered tea ²(   ) into hot water. Aiya was founded about 130 years ago. The company sells matcha both in Japan and overseas. It ³(   ) a range of products, not just tea but also cakes, ice cream among other ⁴(   ). Its efforts have propelled matcha to become a global ⁵(   ). We asked fifth-generation company head Sugita about his business ⁶(   ).

Interview  [4:40]

online video

Checking Key Points

Watch Part 1 and choose the correct answers.

1. You need to whisk the matcha powder in the water to get (creamy foam / distinctive layers).

2. Aiya is located in (Kyoto / Aichi) Prefecture.

3. On tea plantations, sunlight is blocked so that the leaves (remain small / grow bigger) and have a higher umami component.

4. When making matcha, it is important to (remove / use) the stems and veins.

5. Tea leaves are ground into a very fine matcha powder using a (sieve / mortar).

Organizing Information

List the steps in producing matcha powder by completing the table with items from the box below.

	Process of Matcha Tea-Making
1	Tea buds on tea plantations start to grow in April.
2	
3	
4	Steam and dry the leaves.
5	
6	
7	

a. Blow air to separate lighter leaves.
b. Pulverize the leaves and remove the stems and veins with sieves.
c. Cover the tea plants to block the sunlight.
d. Grind the bits of tea leaves into powder using mortars at a factory.
e. Pick the leaves at their peak when they are thin and supple.

Interview

[5:13]

(online / video)

(online / video)

Checking Key Points

Watch Part 2 and choose the correct answers.

1. Compared to the top tea producers in Kyoto, Aiya had (no name recognition / a longer history of matcha production).

2. Aiya decided to make matcha food products because Uji tea producers (were / weren't) doing that.

3. Having increased domestic sales, Aiya entered the (American / Asian) market.

4. At first, it was difficult to sell matcha overseas because it was (not well known / bitter).

5. China and Korea are also producing matcha now, so Sugita is (concerned / pleased).

Organizing Information

Do a SWOT analysis of Aiya's business model by completing the table with items from the box below. (SWOT stands for Strengths, Weaknesses, Opportunities, and Threats.)

Factors	Positive	Negative
Company's internal issues	**S**trengths: • ( ) • ( )	**W**eakness: • ( )
Outside environment	**O**pportunities (90s): • ( ) • ( )	**T**hreat (potential): • ( )

a. Diversification of products

b. Virtually no competitors in the U.S.

c. New original products from other countries

d. The ability to think outside the box

e. Large, untried foreign market

f. Lack of brand recognition

 online video online audio 🎧 DL 17 ◉ CD 17

Confirm the conclusion of the interview by completing the script below.

Sugita: "Don't forget matcha, but go outside of matcha." As matcha starts being used in all different kinds of countries—as people eat it and drink it—I think we'll be seeing matcha in new, different forms and in new and different products. ¹_____ _____ of

what matcha should be and taking a negative approach, I believe it's important to ²_____. We have to take a chance and explore beyond what matcha is. Don't ³_____ _____.

Sharing Our Responses

1. Write down three new facts you learned from the interview. Share them with your partner.

2. With your partner, discuss and decide on a message for each of the following: Takeo Sugita, Aijiro Sugita (the original founder of Aiya), and American consumers. Share your messages with your classmates.

Taking the Next Step

Your marketing team has been ordered to create the next popular matcha-flavored food or drink. As a group, create an advertisement for one of the products from Sharing Our Views 3 on p. 29 or suggest your own original product. Include:

1. The product name, price, and where it will be sold
2. Its attractive points
3. A design for its packaging

Present your product to your classmates. Can you persuade them to stock your product in their shops?

Voice

5

Ayyam Sureau

French Refugee Integration

In this chapter, we'll learn about Ayyam Sureau's effort to assist international refugees in France. Let's find out how she helps them integrate into a new society.

Sharing Our Views

Think about the following questions and talk with your partner.

1. People often say, "When in Rome, do as the Romans do." What do you think this means? Do you agree with this saying? Why or why not?

2. What Japanese customs do you think may be difficult for people visiting Japan to follow?

3. What kind of help do you think you could offer to people moving to your hometown from other countries?

Read this FAQ from an NGO website and answer the True/False questions below. The words in bold will appear in the interview.

FAQ about Refugees

Every day, tens of thousands of people **flee** their homes, becoming **refugees**. One of our responsibilities as global citizens is to understand who refugees are, how they became refugees, and what is being done to assist them.

Q: *Who are they?*

A: Refugees are people who have fled their homes for their own safety. Some are escaping persecution due to their race, religion, social group, sexual orientation, or political beliefs. Others are fleeing violent or **war-torn** cities and countries. Around the world, refugee numbers are **surging**.

Q: *Where do they go?*

A: Some look for shelter within their own countries, and are called internally displaced people (IDPs). **Asylum-seekers** are different; these people escape to another country and apply for protection. If they can prove that they had good reason to leave their homes, they may be **granted refugee status**.

Q: *What kind of help do they get in their new countries?*

A: Refugees can receive legal protection and financial assistance. Germany and France, for example, each receive hundreds of thousands of asylum-seekers every year. Life can be a struggle for them; they may **encounter** culture clashes with the local people they **interact with**. However, in many European countries, there are programs designed to help refugees **integrate** into society. They can enroll in tuition-free classes on financial planning skills, language learning, and even local history.

1. There are more refugees today than there have been in the past.　　T / F

2. Asylum-seekers automatically receive protection in other countries.　　T / F

3. Refugees may be able to take language classes without paying.　　T / F

Boosting Vocabulary

online/audio   DL 19   CD 19

Match these words from the interview with their definitions.

1. acquisition _____   **a.** act of gaining something

2. convert _____   **b.** willing to give help

3. condemn _____   **c.** change character or function

4. generous _____   **d.** get something back

5. regain _____   **e.** disappoint or fail someone or something

6. obligation _____   **f.** moral or legal duty

7. betray _____   **g.** strongly criticize

Introduction   Understanding the Main Topic   ▶ Part 1 0:00-0:48

online/video   online/audio   DL 20   CD 20

1st Listening   Check ☑ the correct statements.

At Sureau's school, _____.

☐ the students are foreign refugees

☐ all are seeking asylum from African nations

☐ there are currently 3,800 students studying

☐ refugees are assisted in a unique way

2nd Listening   Complete the script by filling in the blanks.

Welcome to *Direct Talk*. Today, our guest is Ayyam Sureau. She founded a small school to ¹(   ) refugees in Paris. The number of asylum-seekers in Europe has ²(   ) in recent years, and ³(   ) them into local communities has become a social issue. Over ten years, the school has ⁴(   ) in assisting 3,800 refugees from all over the world, including war-torn Afghanistan, Syria, other parts of the Middle East, African nations, Georgia, and Tibet. This episode examines the unique ⁵(   ) Sureau and her colleagues developed from their experience of welcoming ⁶(   ).

Interview

(online/video)

Checking Key Points

Watch Part 1 and choose the correct answers.

1. Student expenses at this school are (supported by the public / covered by the government).

2. All the graduates either go on to higher education or (find jobs / return to their countries).

3. Students who want to enroll in the school are expected to (take part in various activities / master French within a year).

4. Students learn French by (interacting with locals / taking intensive lessons).

5. The students serve lunch to local people (in the classrooms / at a nearby café).

Organizing Information

Explain Sureau's work with refugees by completing the table. The first letters are provided.

Problem: *What is the problem?*
Integration of ¹(r   ) from other countries into a new ²(c   ) is challenging.
Response: *What did Sureau do in response to the problem?*
She founded a school in Paris to provide a place for refugees and ³(F   ) people to make friends with each other. Students jog, perform plays, sing, and sew together with locals. They also ⁴(p   ) lunch service.
Outcome: *What do the students get out of the experience?*
Through taking part in these ⁵(a   ) with local people, students naturally ⁶(b   ) them.

Interview 2 [5:25]

Checking Key Points

Watch Part 2 and choose the correct answers.

1. Sureau says that it is important for foreigners to (understand the rules of the host country / follow their own cultural norms).

2. Each (student / national group) is assisted by local volunteers who help with their studies.

3. People who help the refugees for charity tend to (continue for a long time / stay for just a short time).

4. Student-volunteer interaction is a way to (help refugees regain trust in other people / push the students to act French).

5. Sureau understands how foreign students feel because she herself is (a refugee from Egypt / a U.S.-born foreigner).

Organizing Information

Describe the Pierre Claver School by completing the table with items from the box below. Some of them are extra.

Philosophy	Refugees need to ¹( ) trust in themselves and others and learn what's considered ²( ) sense in France.
Volunteers	**Who:** From young people to ³( ) **How:** One-on-one instruction
	What: Teach French culture and language, give ⁴( ) on day-to-day life.
Public relations	Student activities ⁵( ) attention from the public, gaining support and ⁶( ).

retirees / advice / encounters / generate / common / regain / obligation / donations

The Words to Live By

▶ **Part 2** 4:02-5:25

(online / video) (online / audio)   DL 21 ⊚ CD 21

Confirm the conclusion of the interview by completing the script below.

Ayyam: Have you heard of the printing technique called *amour* in France? There are letters with ink on one side. And now you print these letters on paper. Sometimes the printed ink is too light. At other times, there is too much ink and the paper gets all black. Ideally, **¹**_____, not blurry or too light. The name of that technique, *amour*, means "love." This is what we should seek. There is no recipe for it. **²**_____ _____. "To love." To love is the root of everything. **³**_____ _____. And there is a journey of love that leads there.

⬗ Sharing Our Responses

1. Write down three new facts you learned from the interview. Share them with your partner.
2. With your partner, discuss and decide on a message for each of the following: Ayyam Sureau, refugees studying at the school, and French volunteers working at the school. Share your messages with your classmates.

⬗ Taking the Next Step

Japan has started to accept more workers from other countries under the Technical Intern Training Program（特定技能実習生制度）. As a group, do an online search for information about the program, including:

1. Its goals
2. Problems some of these interns face in Japan
3. How these problems are tackled

Share your findings with your classmates.

Voice

6

Yuuki Watanabe

The Power of Biologging

In this chapter, we'll learn how scientists use the method of biologging to understand aspects of animal life that have always been mysterious. Let's look at the challenges a scientist has faced in developing biologging devices.

Sharing Our Views

Think about the following questions and talk with your partner.

1. Do you like watching videos of animals showing interesting behaviors? Talk about behaviors you remember.

2. Have you visited any aquariums or zoos? Which ones? What did you like seeing the most?

3. Researching animals is expensive. Do you think the government should help pay for it? Why or why not?

Read the top page of an application for research money and answer the True/False questions below. The words in bold will appear in the interview.

Proud Planet Research Grant Program: Application Form	
Head Researcher	Dr. Bernardo Peres
Organization	Trancoso University
Research Title	Developing Universal **Biologging** Technology
Background	Collecting accurate data on animals in the wild has always been a challenge. Biologging, which involves attaching data-recording **devices** to animals, helps scientists meet that challenge. The idea is not a new one; over 70 years ago, Norwegian researcher Pers Scholander attached an **apparatus** to a whale. The last 20 years have seen crucial **breakthroughs** in this technology, with **astonishingly** small devices **revealing** animal behaviors, movements, and **lifespans**. However, animal-specific **transmitters** are often **complicated** and extremely expensive. In addition, devices can be un**reliable**, resulting in serious research **setbacks**.
Research Plan	The researchers plan to develop and test a **prototype** for a relatively inexpensive universal device by cooperating with biologists studying crows in the U.K., sharks around Japan, and elephants in East Africa. The device will feature a light, strong body, long-lasting batteries, audio and video options, and advanced GPS software. The device will help scientists everywhere collect the data they need.
Amount Requested	US$420,000

1. Dr. Peres hopes to be the first scientist to use biologging with whales.   T / F

2. Biologging can show where animals are as well as how long they live.   T / F

3. The prototype would be tested with animals on land, in water, and in the air.

   T / F

Boosting Vocabulary

online / audio   DL 23   CD 23

Match these words from the interview with their definitions.

1. investigate _____   **a.** get back

2. acceleration _____   **b.** examine, explore

3. retrieve _____   **c.** organized trip for a particular purpose

4. detachment _____   **d.** hunting other animals for food

5. expedition _____   **e.** piece of video recording

6. predatory _____   **f.** increase in speed

7. footage _____   **g.** separation of a small part from the main body

Introduction   Understanding the Main Topic   ▶ Part 1 0:00-0:53

online / video   online / audio   DL 24   CD 24

1st Listening   Check ☑ the correct statements.

Yuuki Watanabe _____.

- ☐ is a biologist specializing in ocean animals
- ☐ is a popular blogger on marine topics
- ☐ shared his findings in a science journal
- ☐ is famous for his investigation on alligators

2nd Listening   Complete the script by filling in the blanks.

Welcome to *Direct Talk*. Our guest today is Yuuki Watanabe, a marine ¹( ). Watanabe is an expert in the rapidly evolving science of biologging. It is a research method that involves placing ²( ) or small cameras on wild animals in order to ³( ) their behaviors and ways of life which are still ⁴( ). Watanabe is particularly well known for his biologging of penguins. He captured never-before-seen footage which was ⁵( ) in the science journal *Nature*. Biologging has revealed some surprising ⁶( ) and Watanabe filled us in on some of those secrets.

Checking Key Points

Watch Part 1 and choose the correct answers.

1. According to Watanabe, before biologging, research on animals was conducted mainly through (observing / capturing) them.

2. Watanabe attaches devices to animals' (heads / backs) to understand what they see.

3. The body temperature of a typical fish is (the same as / higher than) that of its environment.

4. Fish with higher body temperatures can swim (deeper in the sea / at faster speeds) than other fish.

5. From Watanabe's research, it was found that Greenland sharks can most likely live until they are (150 / 400) years old.

Organizing Information

Give an overview of Watanabe's research by completing the table. The first letters are provided.

Previous knowledge	Fish are [1](c). Their bodies are the [2](s) temperature as their environment.
Research question	Why does the body temperature of Great White Sharks increase?
Research method	They compared the [3](s) of different fish.
Findings	Fish with higher body temperatures swim [4](t) to [5](t) times faster. Higher temperatures mean their [6](m) are warm and active.

Interview [5:09]

online video

Checking Key Points

Watch Part 2 and choose the correct answers.

1. Biologging started in the (mid- / late) twentieth century.

2. Watanabe's main difficulty was (attaching devices to / retrieving devices from) Baikal seals.

3. Yasuhiko Naito came up with a new idea and (made a prototype / tried it in the field).

4. It was found that the seals can dive as deep as (223 / 232) meters.

5. Scientists around the world now use the (detach-and-retrieve / recapture-and-retrieve) system.

Organizing Information

Describe Watanabe's team's data collection experiences by completing the table with items from the box below. Some of them are extra.

	Trials	Results
1	Used a "recapturing device" with a timer on the seal. When the timer went off, the device ^{1}(d) a balloon on the seal. The device had a radio ^{2}( ) to help them locate the seal.	The seal swam off somewhere. They lost expensive ^{3}( ).
2	Retrieved the device by tying a rope around on the seals and ^{4}(**ing**) in the rope.	The data was not ^{5}( ) because the seal needed to drag the heavy ropes.
3	Put a timed ^{6}( ) mechanism on the devices and retrieved only the devices.	Hard data was successfully collected.

detachment / inflate / equipment / pull / transmitter / release / reveal / reliable

The Words to Live By

Part 2 4:18–5:09

online video online audio DL 25 CD 25

Confirm the conclusion of the interview by completing the script below.

Watanabe: "The heart of the matter." Doing research that uses biologging means
1 _____ . It's not just about going
to the South Pole and slapping a machine on the animals there. If you ask me,
2 _____ .

I'm trying to get right to the heart of this giant framework called biology—in other words,
3 _____ .

Forget the insignificant details. My goal is to get right to the heart of the matter.

Sharing Our Responses

1. Write down three new facts you learned from the interview. Share them with your partner.
2. With your partner, discuss and decide on a message for each of the following: Watanabe, a Baikal seal, and future biologgers.

Taking the Next Step

You are a biologist and want to do biologging research on two similar animals. In pairs, go online and complete the chart below. Compare and contrast the animals.

Animal		
Habitat		
Lifespan		
Food		
Behaviors		
Other		
What could you find out if you attached biologging devices on these animals?		

Share your findings with your classmates who work at your research center.

46

Voice

7

Cherrie Atilano

Farming Is the Future

In this chapter, we'll witness a farmer-entrepreneur's passion for invigorating farming in the Philippines. Let's see how she demonstrates that farming is not a "one-way ticket to poverty" but can be a profitable and rewarding business.

Sharing Our Views

Think about the following questions and talk with your partner.

1. Have you ever grown any fruits or vegetables?
   Yes: When? What kinds?
   No: Are you interested in growing your own food? Why or why not?

2. Do you check where the fruits and vegetables you eat are grown? Why or why not?

3. The number of Japanese farmers has been decreasing. Why do you think this is happening?

Read this introduction page to a Filipino agriculture textbook and answer the True/False questions below. The words in bold will appear in the interview.

Farming in the Philippines: Facing Today's Reality

Rice and sugar. Coffee and pineapples. Mangoes and bananas. These are just some of the foods grown here in the Philippines. Outside the major cities, **massive** plantations and **small-scale** farms seem to be everywhere, projecting an image that our economy relies primarily on agriculture. This **notion**, however, is increasingly **disconnected** from reality.

There is evidence that rice was being grown here at least 5,000 years ago. Over the centuries, new plants were brought by people settling here, but farming, **in itself**, changed little. By the time Spain colonized the Philippines, the main practice was still **subsistence** farming. The Spanish colonial period, stretching from 1565 until 1898, saw increased rice, sugarcane, tobacco, abacá, and coconut farming. The Spanish also introduced crops from their territories in the Americas, including corn, potatoes, sweet potatoes, and tomatoes. The U.S. took control from 1898 until WWII, introducing **schemes** for expanding and mechanizing food production.

Agriculture is still vital to our country, but the current trend is discouraging. Only about a quarter of all Filipino workers are now engaged in farming. Many of our farmers are aging, but still lack basic skills and training. In addition, much agricultural land is being turned into golf courses, resorts, and industrial parks.

This textbook invites you to **reflect on** ways to address these and other concerns at both local and national levels. Farming is the key to our food security, and we hope you will be **inspired** to make a difference and protect our agricultural **legacy**.

1. The American colonial period followed the Spanish colonial period.   T / F

2. Around 75% of Filipino workers are farmers who need more training.   T / F

3. The author concludes that the Philippines should shift its focus from agriculture to other industries.   T / F

Boosting Vocabulary

 online audio   DL 27   CD 27

Match these words from the interview with their definitions.

1. eradicate _____
2. fertilizer _____
3. cooperative _____
4. venture _____
5. economies of scale _____
6. inclusive _____
7. fortitude _____

a. mental or emotional strength
b. broad, covering many things
c. jointly owned enterprise or organization
d. substance that makes soil richer
e. proceed despite possible danger
f. reduction of costs as a result of mass-producing
g. do away with completely, get rid of

Introduction   Understanding the Main Topic   ▶ Part 1 0:00–0:51

online video   online audio  DL 28   CD 28

 **1st Listening   Check ☑ the correct statements.**

Cherrie Atilano _____.

- ☐ is a professor of sustainable agriculture
- ☐ helps farmers to improve their earnings
- ☐ wants to encourage young people
- ☐ is not yet recognized outside of her country

 **2nd Listening   Complete the script by filling in the blanks.**

Welcome to *Direct Talk*—interviews with leaders, visionaries, and pioneers who are shaping Asia and the rest of the world. Cherrie Atilano is a Filipino [1](   ) and social entrepreneur [2](   ) to make farming a profession that's attractive and respected. She trains and advises [3](   ) farmers on how to improve their income and productivity. She runs her own business with a focus on sustainable [4](   ) to inspire young people that farming can be their future. Atilano's work has won her numerous national and international [5](   ). She asks us to reflect on how farming is key to sustaining and [6](   ) our lives—lives of all human beings.

Part 1 [4:11]

online / video

Checking Key Points

Watch Part 1 and choose the correct answers.

1. Atilano founded AGREA, which aims to demonstrate how (profitable / technological) farming can be.

2. AGREA's model farm teaches farmers to (sell organic products / make use of what they have) as sustainable practices.

3. In many parts of the Philippines, food must be imported due to the (colonial legacy / government policy) of mono-crop plantations.

4. Atilano found that the only part of the coconut that farmers were exporting was the (copra / sugar).

5. Atilano helped local coconut farmers to (form a cooperative / adopt a new crop).

Organizing Information

Explain Atilano's work with one community by completing the table with items from the box below. Some of them are extra.

What had the community been producing?	Copra, the dried meat of the coconut
What was the problem?	Copra is very [1]( ) in value.
What did they do to increase their income?	They diversified their products and produced coconut [2]( ).
What did Atilano help to set up?	A [3]( ) made up of 30 families
What is the advantage of a cooperative?	It increases the [4]( ) of scale. As a legal entity, it can get [5]( ) support.

cooperative / economies / fertilizers / government
high / plantation / low / sugar

Interview Part 2 [3:56]

online / video

Checking Key Points

Watch Part 2 and choose the correct answers.

1. Atilano is trying to introduce (fair trade practices / foreign investors) to rural communities.

2. Atilano's father was a (poor plantation farmer / sugar plantation manager).

3. AGREA runs a school where farmers can learn about (organic farming / basic trading) in one month.

4. One of the major missions of the school is to (help poor farmers get certificates / keep young people in farming).

5. Atilano says that supermarket culture (disconnects people from nature / makes farming seem attractive).

Organizing Information

Describe the roles AGREA plays by completing the chart. The first letters are provided.

Operate a model farm:
Teach simple and profitable techniques such as creating organic fertilizers.

Organize cooperatives:
Help cooperatives manage their business and get government support.

AGREA's Roles

Promote ^{1}(f   ) (   ):
Reduce the number of traders and treat both producers and ^{2}(c   ) with fairness.

Run a ^{3}(s   ):
Teach ^{4}(o   ) farming.
Award ^{5}(c   ) for completion.

(online / **video**) (online / **audio**) 🎧 DL 29 ⊙ CD 29

Confirm the conclusion of the interview by completing the script below.

Atilano: I always believe that when people would see dirt and soil, I see gold because I see that farming is a good business. You know,

1_____

that you can have. It will teach you things that are not in the books. It will teach you things that you cannot get in the four corner[s] of your classrooms. It will teach you

2_____. Farming is a place where I learn so much. It's always my happy place, you know. It's a gift to make other people dream how to be more hopeful, **3**_____

_____, and how to make them dream for the community. "Farming is life."

Sharing Our Responses

1. Write down three new facts you learned from the interview. Share them with your partner.
2. With your partner, discuss and decide on a message for each of the following: Cherrie Atilano, Atilano's father, and young Filipino students in AGREA. Share your messages with your classmates.

Taking the Next Step

Japan's population of farmers is also aging and shrinking. As a group, list reasons making farming an attractive career choice for today's youth. You can refer to AGREA's website. Include:

1. Why farming is important to Japan
2. Cooperatives and new ventures in Japan
   - Who they are and what they grow
   - What they do to make farming more attractive

Present your proposal to your classmates. Can you persuade them to become farmers?

Voice

8

Luciano Benetton

New Challenges for a Fashion Giant

In this chapter, we'll learn about Luciano Benetton's commitment to promoting diversity and integration. Let's find out how he advertises his fashion brand and how he communicates his beliefs about the way the world should be.

Sharing Our Views

Think about the following questions and talk with your partner.

1. Look at what you and your partner are wearing. What do your clothes say about you?

2. What's the oldest piece of clothing you own? How old is it? Why have you kept it?

3. Rank the following from 1 (most important to you) to 4 (least important to you) when buying clothes:
   [   ] brand name   [   ] design
   [   ] comfort   [   ] price

 online audio DL 30 CD 30

Read this top page of a sustainable lifestyle website and answer the True/False questions below. The words in bold will appear in the interview.

Weighing the Options: Fast Fashion

"Cute shorts—and they're cheap! Oh, and they've got black T-shirts—I should get one. Or maybe two? And a couple of white ones…"

Does this sound like you when you're shopping? If so, you're the target customer for "fast fashion." This term refers to the affordable, mass-produced clothing we see online and in **virtually** every shopping street and outlet mall. This trend started over 20 years ago and **has taken the world by storm**.

The pros of fast fashion are easy to see. If your favorite style blogger says that **vibrant** oranges are going to replace last year's **understated** pinks and beiges, you can order an orange jacket online today and have it delivered tomorrow. And if you're looking for the perfect combination of **brand recognition** and reasonable prices, some **iconic** labels have introduced fast fashion lines that **coexist** with their higher-end items.

But there are some serious cons as well. For one thing, the pressure to produce clothing quickly **contributes** to stressful and dangerous factory work. For another, we are **being swept along** by a "throwaway culture" trend: people wearing clothes just once before throwing them away. Worldwide, millions of tons of clothing are discarded annually by consumers.

Some companies are **setting an example** by improving labor practices and reducing their environmental impact. However, for us to **tackle** the disadvantages of fast fashion, it is **vital** that customers understand the effects of buying that extra pair of shorts or yet another T-shirt.

1. Fast-fashion shopping can be done both on the Internet and in stores.   T / F

2. Workers in fast-fashion factories often face terrible working conditions.   T / F

3. The writer feels that it is the responsibility of the companies, not the consumers, to deal with the problems of fast fashion.   T / F

Boosting Vocabulary

Match these words from the interview with their definitions.

1. distribution _____
2. market _____
3. convey _____
4. diversity _____
5. admission _____
6. exhibition _____
7. compile _____

a. system of delivering orders or supplies
b. the right to enter a place, event, or organization
c. public showing
d. variety, having different elements
e. promote a product or service
f. communicate, express
g. collect and edit

Introduction

Understanding the Main Topic   ▶ Part 1 0:00-0:58

 **Check ☑ the correct statements.**

Luciano Benetton _____.

☐ is one of the founders of an apparel maker
☐ first became well known in the 1990s
☐ runs a social welfare business for youths
☐ has joined the fashion division again

 **Complete the script by filling in the blanks.**

Welcome to *Direct Talk*—interviews with leaders, visionaries, and pioneers who are shaping Asia and the rest of the world. Luciano Benetton took the world by storm in the 1980s as ¹(   ) of the iconic apparel maker that bears his name. Benetton gained worldwide attention with colorful, youthful products and ²(   ) tackling social issues. Beyond ³(   ), the company now runs restaurants, does agriculture, and is even involved in ⁴(   ) (   ). After a time away from fashion and now in his 80s, Luciano Benetton is back in the apparel ⁵(   ): a man forever looking to the younger generation. We spoke with the fashion ⁶(   ) on his latest efforts.

Checking Key Points

Watch Part 1 and choose the correct answers.

1. Luciano wants to rebuild his company by (following / going against) the current fast-fashion trends.

2. The Benetton brand started in (Treviso / Venice).

3. With her brothers' help, Giuliana Benetton began selling (knitted clothing / kids' clothing) in 1955.

4. In contrast to most Italian fashion in the 1950s, Benetton's products were (understated / colorful).

5. Luciano learned about business through (overseas sales networks / relationships he formed in his hometown).

Organizing Information

Describe highlights in Benetton's life and career by completing the table.

1935	Luciano was born in ^{1}( ).
From 1955	• Luciano, along with his brothers, started selling the ^{2}( ) that his sister Giuliana was making. • Benetton's clothing appealed to the ^{3}( ) generation. • Its reputation for ^{4}( ) and comfort helped the company grow.
1980s	Benetton took the world by storm.
Now	• The industry is being swept along by ^{5}( ) fashion. • Luciano returned to the ^{6}( ) division.

Interview Part 2 [5:02]

Checking Key Points

Watch Part 2 and choose the correct answers.

1. In expanding overseas, Benetton changed its (products / ads) slightly to meet local demand.

2. Benetton's marketing strategy was to advertise (the company itself / individual products).

3. Benetton ads (raise funds to solve / send messages about) global social problems.

4. Students admitted to Fabrica are given (travel and living expenses / job opportunities there).

5. Imago Mundi is a project that (collects works of art from around the world / creates an ideal image of fashion).

Organizing Information

Explain Benetton's work for global diversity by completing the table with items from the box below. Some of them are extra.

"All the colors in the world"	This is one of Benneton's ad ^{1}( ) showing diversity and peaceful coexistence. Benetton's ads have since ^{2}( ) global social issues such as racial discrimination, ethnic ^{3}( ), and human rights.
Fabrica	This is a school training talented young ^{4}( ) from around the world. Students can transcend national and cultural barriers here.
Imago Mundi	This is a project providing opportunities to artists from all over the world. **Collection:** - ^{5}( ) into catalogs by country and region - 25,000 works from 168 areas - Can be viewed in ^{6}( ) or online

admitted / artists / campaigns / compiled / conflicts / exhibitions / retail / tackled

Confirm the conclusion of the interview by completing the script below.

Luciano: We have to ¹_____

_____,

from less wealthy countries to enable them to participate in a collective under equal conditions with everyone else. In each area of the world, we find ²_____

_____. "With art—with artists—there are no borders;

³_____." I also believe that this is a message

for young people.

Sharing Our Responses

1. Write down three new facts you learned from the interview. Share them with your partner.

2. With your partner, discuss and decide on a message for each of the following: Luciano Benetton, a customer shopping for fast fashion, and a student at Fabrica. Share your messages with your classmates.

Taking the Next Step

You work in the advertising department of an apparel maker. Your job is to create an ad that promotes the company's products while reflecting its core values.

1. With your group, decide: Who is your target customer? What kinds of clothes will attract them? What social message do you want to send?

2. Create your ad. Include:
    - Your campaign slogan
    - A picture of the new clothing items being promoted
    - The company logo

3. Practice presenting your ad, then present it to another group. Can you persuade them to buy your items?

Voice

9

Viola Cheng

Helping the Socially Vulnerable

In this chapter, we'll learn about the unique business model a young entrepreneur has created in managing popular restaurants. Let's look at her commitment to helping socially vulnerable people.

Sharing Our Views

Think about the following questions and talk with your partner.

1. What kinds of people do you consider to be socially vulnerable?

2. Who should be responsible for helping them?

3. Do you know of any businesses that help them? Which ones? What do they provide?

Read this flier from a recruitment agency and answer the True/False questions below. The words in bold will appear in the interview.

Dear small business owner,

Over the last five years, the city of Springfield has seen significant economic growth. Three major companies have moved their headquarters to our city, and average incomes here continue to rise.

With all this good news, it's easy to forget that the number of **socially vulnerable** people here in Springfield is also getting higher. Some are physically challenged or have mental health issues. Others are victims of **domestic violence**. And some immigrants lack the English skills necessary to achieve **socio-economic** stability. All of them are at risk of falling through the **cracks**.

Here at Hire a Heart, we understand that your business needs to **make a profit**. But we also know that **socially responsible** business owners like you are looking for ways to give back to the community. Hire a Heart is **committed** to helping you identify and hire **disadvantaged** people who are ready and willing to be your best employees. Everyone registered with Hire a Heart comes highly recommended by a **social worker** and has undergone a background check. Here's how Hire a Heart made a difference in one Springfield citizen's life:

 *Clara: By the time I recovered from surgery on my foot, I had lost my job and was deep in **debt**. I was getting my monthly **welfare** check, but that wasn't nearly enough. I was getting **desperate**! Thanks to Hire a Heart, I have regular **income** doing factory work I really enjoy. Last month, I was made a **supervisor**!*

Whether you're just starting out as an entrepreneur or you've been part of Springfield's commercial life for years, contact Hire a Heart for your recruiting needs!

1. Springfield is experiencing a period of economic downturn.   T / F

2. A language barrier can be an obstacle to getting and keeping a job.   T / F

3. By registering with Hire a Heart, Clara was able to find a job.   T / F

Boosting Vocabulary

 online audio DL 35 CD 35

Match these words from the interview with their definitions.

1. disparity ____
2. orphanage ____
3. institution ____
4. prospect ____
5. isolate ____
6. steady ____
7. accomplish ____

a. stable, continuing for a period of time
b. unfair difference or gap
c. possibility, expectation
d. organization, facility
e. home for children without parents
f. achieve
g. separate from others

Introduction

Understanding the Main Topic ▶ Part 1 0:00–0:47

online video online audio DL 36 CD 36

 **1st Listening** Check ☑ the correct statements.

Viola Cheng ____.

☐ runs a traditional Chinese restaurant
☐ manages a company in Taiwan
☐ mainly hires recent college graduates
☐ considers training at her restaurants to be very important

 2nd Listening Complete the script by filling in the blanks.

Welcome to *Direct Talk*—interviews with leaders, visionaries, and pioneers who are shaping Asia and the rest of the world. Today's guest is Viola Cheng, a young Taiwanese entrepreneur whose ¹( ) management style is attracting attention. Cheng is the CEO of a company that runs restaurant chains and is ²( ) to hiring people with ³( ) backgrounds. She firmly believes that ⁴( ) workers with a ⁵( ) income and training them with useful work skills enables them to get ahead in life. She also shared why she feels businesses should be more socially ⁶( ).

Interview Part 1 [4:20]

Checking Key Points

Watch Part 1 and choose the correct answers.

1. The gap between high and low incomes has been (narrowing / widening) in Taiwan in recent years.

2. Cheng expects the workers at her restaurants to (have prior business skills / develop skills through experience).

3. About (one-third / two-thirds) of the workers at Cheng's restaurants are from disadvantaged backgrounds.

4. Cheng's sister-in-law brings her experience and personal connections as a (social worker / business entrepreneur).

5. A company that is widely recognized for its (good customer service / contribution to society) may be certified as a B Corporation.

Organizing Information

Describe Cheng's business model by completing the table. Some first letters are provided.

The chain restaurants	- Serving ramen noodles and other Japanese dishes - Eight locations in and around Taipei
Mission	- Providing jobs to help the socially [1](v) - Giving them work experience and [2](s)
Employees	- More than 60% from [3](d) backgrounds **Examples:** (*add three or more to the list*) ・single-parent families ・ _____ ・ _____ ・ _____
Recruitment	**In charge:** Sister-in-law - Contacts [4](o) such as family support centers - Finds people who are looking for [5](e)

62

Interview

[4:57]

Checking Key Points

Watch Part 2 and choose the correct answers.

1. When Cheng was a child, she learned from her (teacher / mother) to donate to institutions.

2. During her university years, Cheng realized the importance of helping people in need by (offering frequent donations / changing their situations).

3. Cheng believes business owners should (use part of their revenue / be required to hire socially vulnerable workers) to contribute to a society.

4. Cheng visits her restaurants (every day / once a week) to train the employees.

5. The workers at Cheng's restaurants (have a chance to manage the restaurant / need to find work elsewhere after their contracts end).

Organizing Information

Retell Ru Lichi's story by completing the summary with items from the box below. Some of them are extra.

When my husband's business ¹(   ), we struggled with a lot of ²(   ). My children were still in school, so I desperately needed to work. Because I had no work experience, I had no ³(   ) of finding a job. But luckily, I got a job at Viola Cheng's company! There, I was able to earn a ⁴(   ) income and that brought ⁵(   ) back to my life. By going through the training she gave me, I am now a ⁶(   ) at one of her restaurants. I am so thankful to her.

debts / prospect / donations / isolated / steady
failed / manager / improved / stability

63

Confirm the conclusion of the interview by completing the script below.

Cheng: So this is my favorite phrase: ¹"_____

and accomplish your goals." I interpret it
to mean that we should always be thinking
about other people, whether in our personal
lives or through what we do for work. If we
face the world with sincerity, do our best, and

² _____,

maybe then we can ³ _____

_____ to do good as well.

Sharing Our Responses

1. Write down three new facts you learned from the interview. Share them with your partner.

2. With your partner, discuss and decide on a message for one of the following: Viola Cheng, workers at Cheng's restaurants, and a business owner who wants to help others. Share your messages with your classmates.

Taking the Next Step

You have decided to hire several disadvantaged workers at your restaurant. None of them has any work experience. What kind of training will you give them? As a group, create a training program to help them succeed at their new jobs. Include:

1. The type of restaurant
2. How many you're hiring and for what jobs: cook, assistant cook, waiter, other
3. A training schedule, including skills they need and how long the training will last

Share your program with other groups. Did you come up with ideas they can borrow for their own training programs?

Voice

10

Meik Wiking

The Danish Recipe for Happiness

In this chapter, we'll learn why Denmark is ranked among the top countries on the Happiness Index. Let's learn from a leading researcher how our sense of happiness can be influenced by social media as well.

Sharing Our Views

Think about the following questions and talk with your partner.

1. When do you feel happiest?

2. What is your definition of a happy life?

3. How do other people's happy posts on social media affect you?

Read this magazine article and answer the True/False questions below. The words in bold will appear in the interview.

Unhappy? Put Down Your Smartphone!

Everyone **strives for** happiness and **well-being**, but how do we know whether we have achieved them? Is there a way to measure how happy we are as a nation? Researchers seeking answers to these questions **conduct** extensive worldwide surveys and use the **numerical** data coming out of them to rank countries according to happiness. These rankings are published in annual reports, worrying some and reassuring others.

According to the reports, we Americans should be concerned; happiness levels among both adolescents and adults here have been gradually falling for at least 20 years. It is true that violent crime and unemployment rates have dropped and that income is higher. However, the time we spend staring at screens and being **bombarded** by social media messages is **undermining** our **quality of life**. Our limited face-to-face interaction with others is an **indicator** of how **isolated** we have become.

On the other hand, the Nordic countries (Denmark, Finland, Iceland, Norway, and Sweden) are **consistently** ranked among the world's happiest. Some experts point to these countries' social support systems and to political equality as major factors contributing to **sustaining** a happy society.

By learning from the Nordic example and **deliberately** working to reestablish relationships with people that we trust, we Americans may be able to take control of our happiness... and score higher on next year's report.

1. Many participate in happiness research by answering survey questions. T / F

2. Better working conditions have led to increased American happiness. T / F

3. The author believes that Americans can learn from the Nordic countries. T / F

Boosting Vocabulary

 online / audio   DL 39   CD 39

Match these words from the interview with their definitions.

1. exceed _____   **a.** suffering, grief

2. livelihood _____   **b.** people used for comparison in an experiment

3. misery _____   **c.** go beyond the limits of, be greater than

4. release _____   **d.** compared to others

5. relative _____   **e.** means of support

6. control group _____   **f.** announce, publish

7. reinforce _____   **g.** strengthen, emphasize

Introduction   Understanding the Main Topic   ▶ Part 1 0:00–0:53

 online / video    online / audio   DL 40   CD 40

 **1st Listening**   Check ☑ the correct statements.

Meik Wiking _____.

☐ is the author of a popular book

☐ writes about Danish cooking

☐ works to improve a welfare system

☐ explains the idea of *hygge*

 **2nd Listening**   Complete the script by filling in the blanks.

Welcome to *Direct Talk*—interviews with leaders, visionaries, and pioneers who are shaping Asia and the rest of the world. Today, our guest is Meik Wiking of Denmark. In recent years, his country has become known as the happiest place on the ¹( ). One reason is thought to be the ²( ) social services available to its citizens. Another is their unique ³( ) of *hygge*, which translates to coziness or to create a comfortable, familiar ⁴( ). Wiking has written a book on the subject; it has been a huge hit worldwide. He spoke to us on life in a ⁵( ) state, *hygge*, and the Danish ⁶( ) for happiness.

Checking Key Points

Watch Part 1 and choose the correct answers.

1. Wiking explains that Denmark's social welfare system aims to (reduce extreme unhappiness / maximize individual job satisfaction).

2. The 2012 U.N. happiness report was based on (GDP and other economic factors / issues surrounding quality of life).

3. Wiking founded a (Danish cultural center / happiness research institute).

4. A comfortable *hygge* atmosphere is created (by / without) making a deliberate effort.

5. According to Wiking, (buying things / dinner plans with friends) is an example of a *hygge*-ly situation.

Organizing Information

Give an overview of Denmark by completing the table with items from the box below. Some of them are extra.

Population	¹( ) million
Land area	Mostly ²( )
Food self-sufficiency rate	More than ³( )%
Energy resources	Known for green energy, for example ⁴( ) power
Income tax rates	⁵( )% or more
Happiness ranking (2012)	Number one out of more than ⁶( ) countries
Support systems	Access to health care, ⁷( ) market for women, university education

5.7 / 50 / 57 / 150 / 300 / farmland / labor / lowland / nuclear / wind

Interview Part 2 [4:39]

Checking Key Points

Watch Part 2 and choose the correct answers.

1. Danish ideas of relaxing may seem (lazy / unrealistic) to outsiders.

2. The Job Satisfaction Index shows that (the wages people receive / social relationships in the workplace) have more influence on job satisfaction.

3. Wiking says that (the country's social welfare system / support from his family) gave him the courage to create a company.

4. Wiking claims that exposure to others' happy posts on social media can (boost your motivation / make you unhappy).

5. In Wiking's experiment, the treatment group took a break from social (media / gatherings).

Organizing Information

Describe Wiking's social media experiment by completing the table.

Hypothesis	Social media influences how people feel about happiness.
Procedure	**Step 1:** Conducted happiness [1]( ) of 1,100 people **Step 2:** Assigned the people randomly into two groups [2]( ) **Group** — Continued as usual ⟷ **Treatment Group** — Took a one-week break from [3]( ) **Step 3:** Repeated Step 1 and compared the results
Result	People in the treatment group showed [4]( ) happiness levels.
Conclusion	The philosophy of [5]( ) is needed worldwide.

69

(online / video)   (online / audio)   🎧 DL 41   💿 CD 41

Confirm the conclusion of the interview by completing the script below.

Wiking: So I've written, "Good conditions for good lives" because I think that is ¹_____ _____. I think that's what governments should aim for. I think that's what workplaces should aim for. There will be unhappiness. ²_____

_____. There will be heartbreak. There will be worry. And—but let's find out how we can design cities, workplaces, societies ³_____ _____ of a good life.

Sharing Our Responses

1. Write down three new facts you learned from the interview. Share them with your partner.

2. With your partner, discuss and decide on a message for each of the following: Meik Wiking, someone who feels guilty for relaxing, and a friend who feels isolated by others' social media posts. Share your messages with your classmates.

Taking the Next Step

As a group of researchers, conduct a happiness survey and present your findings.

1. List ten things you think make people happy.
2. Each group member should interview three classmates outside the group.
   - Ask each interviewee to rank the top three items on your list.
   - Assign points for each answer: 3 points for the top item, and 2 and 1 for the other two items.
3. Back in your group, compile all your group's interviewee answers.
4. Create a pie chart illustrating your data. Label each section and give your chart a title.
5. Present your chart to the class. Is your data similar to other groups' data?

Tamako Mitarai

Knitting the Future by Hand

In this chapter, we'll learn about an entrepreneur's endeavor to create jobs for women in a Japanese city devastated by the 2011 earthquake and tsunami. Let's find out what business model she has used to help her company succeed in its mission.

Sharing Our Views

Think about the following questions and talk with your partner.

1. Do you own any handmade items of clothing or accessories?

    Yes: How are they different from factory-made items?

    No: What is your image of handmade clothes and accessories?

2. If you were to establish your own business, what would you like it to be?

3. What would the benefits be of owning your own business? What would the challenges be?

Read this feature article from an in-flight magazine and answer the True/False questions below. The words in bold will appear in the interview.

Love in Every Stitch

The diamond **stitch**. The cable stitch. The tree of life stitch. Each unique, each beautiful, and each a part of the rich culture of the fisherman's sweater. The fisherman's sweater was probably first knitted in Guernsey, an island in the English Channel. Fishing was an important part of Guernsey's trade, and the fishermen needed clothing that would be warm, strong, easy to move in, and would keep out water. To meet these needs, their wives developed the "gansa," a simple navy-blue sweater. Over time, the **textured patterns** became more complicated. Knitters in Scotland and Ireland developed new stitches that covered the entire sweater.

One version of the gansa, in particular, has **made a reputation** for itself: the "Aran jumper" from the Aran Islands in western Ireland. The first Aran jumpers were likely knit in the late 1890s or early 1900s. Knitters were highly skilled; one sweater might have 100,000 stitches and take three to six weeks to complete.

In the 1950s, an Irish singing group appeared on American television wearing fisherman's sweaters, starting a new fashion trend. People back in Ireland saw the **potential** for handmade sweaters to **make a profit** and knitting them became a **viable** industry. Several new sweater brands were introduced, **generating** much-needed income for Aran Islands residents.

Aran jumpers continue to be in **high demand**; customers feel that the **one-of-a-kind** patterns and high quality **justify** the steep prices they pay. Many say they feel the love in every stitch.

1. Gansa sweaters were created for Guernsey women to wear.   T / F

2. Knitting a sweater might take up to a month and a half.   T / F

3. Aran jumpers all feature the same basic pattern of stitches.   T / F

Boosting Vocabulary

online audio 🎧 DL 43 ◎ CD 43

Match these words from the interview with their definitions.

1. revitalize   _____
2. launch   _____
3. endeavor   _____
4. stagnate   _____
5. originate   _____
6. defect   _____
7. dignity   _____

a. stay the same
b. give new life or energy
c. quality of deserving respect
d. begin something, put into operation
e. serious effort, attempt
f. start, come from a particular place
g. failure, problem

Introduction   Understanding the Main Topic   ▶ Part 1 0:00–0:49

online video   online audio   🎧 DL 44   ◎ CD 44

 **1st Listening**   Check ☑ the correct statements.

Tamako Mitarai _____.

☐ is the vice president of a company

☐ once worked at a Japanese consulting firm

☐ had a job in a foreign country

☐ sells high-quality, hand-knitted products

2nd Listening   Complete the script by filling in the blanks.

Welcome to *Direct Talk*. Our guest today is Tamako Mitarai, CEO of Kesennuma Knitting. She used to work at a foreign consulting firm and also spent a year as a ¹( ) to Bhutan's prime minister. Her company's products include sweaters, cardigans, and other ²( ) hand-knitted by the women of Kesennuma, a region ³( ) by the 2011 Tohoku earthquake and tsunami. Her high-end products sell for around 150,000 yen apiece, but they have been popular, serving as a ⁴( ) business model for ⁵( ) a region through handmade goods. We asked Mitarai about her business ⁶( ).

Checking Key Points

Watch Part 1 and choose the correct answers.

1. Kesennuma Knitting (was launched in / was relocated to) Miyagi in 2012.

2. The products have been so popular that there is now (a wait-list / an online fan forum).

3. Mitarai believed that for the endeavor to be sustainable, she needed to (generate a profit for the company / provide local women with full-time jobs).

4. Mitarai's unique approach was to set the price first, then the (working conditions of the knitters / quality of the knitwear).

5. Each sweater is given a (unique ID / name tag), so if it is sent in for repairs, the staff can quickly identify which yarn to use.

Organizing Information

Describe Kesennuma Knitting's business model by completing the infographic.

Sweater features:
1 _____
_____

Knitters: 2 _____

Materials used:
3 _____

Services

Before:
4 _____
_____

During:
5 _____
_____

After:
6 _____
_____

Interview  [5:59] (online video)

Checking Key Points

Watch Part 2 and choose the correct answers.

1. Many locals in Kesennuma say that they learned how to knit from their (fathers / mothers).

2. The knitters work (from 9:00 to 5:00 every day / at their own pace).

3. The knitters are paid a certain amount for (each piece of knitwear / each hour they spend knitting).

4. If Mitarai finds any defects when inspecting the finished knitwear, the item is (partially mended / undone and re-knitted).

5. When customers place orders with Kesennuma Knitting, they expect something that (will last them a lifetime / is very trendy).

Organizing Information

Explain the development of Kesennuma Knitting by completing the table with items from the box below. Some of them are extra.

Before 2011	The local industries had ¹( ).
2011	Mitarai started to work as a consultant for local Kesennuma ²( ).
2012	She became the CEO of Kesennuma Knitting, hoping to ³( ) the locals with work.
(In between)	• She hired knitters with various skill levels so that everyone could ⁴( ). • The company was able to make a ⁵( ).
2016	She started accepting ⁶( ) from outside the disaster area to build a business free of the "natural disaster" image.

provide / stagnated / profit / endeavor
applications / authorities / volunteers / contribute

Confirm the conclusion of the interview by completing the script below.

Mitarai: My hope is that this company becomes a future classic—an old, time-honored business. In Japan, we have quite a number of companies that have more than 200 years—even 500 years of history. Companies like that usually have great customers. The company is ¹_____. Their food is usually amazing, or their products are really great. Most of them are run by an owner who oversees all operations, who ²_____ _____. That successor could be their own child, or it could be somebody they trust. In the sense of ³_____

_____,
these old Japanese businesses provide a blueprint. I want this company to have a global reputation. I want for us to be synonymous with quality sweaters.

Sharing Our Responses

1. Write down three new facts you learned from the interview. Share them with your partner.

2. With your partner, discuss and decide on a message for each of the following: Tamako Mitarai, the Kesennuma knitters, and potential Kesennuma customers. Share your messages with your classmates.

Taking the Next Step

In a group, list your hometowns and businesses in them that need to be revitalized. Choose one from the group and create a website top page to promote a new company and its products. You can refer to the Kesennuma Knitting's website as reference. Include:

1. What your products are
2. Who the workers are and what they do
3. How your company hopes to benefit the local area

After practicing, present your top page to your classmates. Can you persuade them to buy your goods?

Voice

12

Sun Xiaolong

Towards a Zero-Waste Future

In this chapter, we'll learn about some of the challenges of managing waste in Singapore. Let's learn about how one scientist there is trying to meet these challenges by eliminating toxic wastes.

Sharing Our Views

Think about the following questions and talk with your partner.

1. How do you feel about paying for plastic bags when shopping?

2. How do you sort your garbage before throwing it away?

3. What do you do to reduce waste?

Read this excerpt from an urban planning textbook and answer the True/False questions below. The words in bold will appear in the interview.

Zero Waste: From Fantasy to Reality

One topic that comes up in discussions about **pollution**'s impact on the environment is "zero waste." This term describes a situation where all products are absorbed back into a system without producing extra or unnecessary waste.

For most of human history, zero waste was a way of life; **relatively** few people could afford to throw things away without reusing them. For decades, however, we have discarded higher and higher **volumes** of trash, sending it to **incineration plants** and **dumping** the **ash** into **landfills**. The more trash we **generate**, the more **pressing** the **issue** of disposal becomes. Reversing this trend feels, to many, like a fantasy.

Hoping to turn fantasy into reality, Paul Palmer started Zero Waste Systems Inc. in the early 1970s. His motivation was to **deal with** industrial waste, not by **disposing** of or recycling it, but by "repurposing" it—using it in other ways. Since then, several other zero-waste companies have started handling both chemical and food waste. Governments have also gotten involved. Singapore, for example, declared 2019 the "Year Towards Zero Waste" and scientists there are **taking a closer look at** ways to handle **toxic substances** in incinerated ash.

In recent years, several popular how-to books have come out, **encouraging** readers to cook zero-waste meals, achieve zero-waste homes, and live zero-waste lives. Given this **surge** of interest at the corporate, government, and individual levels, are permanent solutions **just around the corner**?

1. Landfills are an example of zero-waste trash management.   T / F

2. Palmer's idea was to avoid throwing away industrial waste.   T / F

3. There is plenty of advice about how we can all reduce waste.   T / F

Boosting Vocabulary

online audio   DL 47   CD 47

Match these words from the interview with their definitions.

1. littering _____
2. plant _____
3. uninhabited _____
4. accumulate _____
5. solidify _____
6. solution _____
7. contaminate _____

a. place where an industrial process takes place
b. change from a liquid or gas to a hard mass
c. liquid mixture
d. dropping trash on the ground
e. pile up, gather
f. make impure or unclean
g. having no residents

Introduction   Understanding the Main Topic   ▶ Part 1 0:00-0:50

online video   online audio   DL 48   CD 48

1st Listening   Check ☑ the correct statements.

Sun Xiaolong _____.

- ☐ is the manager of a metal-pressing factory
- ☐ is trying to treat harmful waste
- ☐ collects rare metals from industrial waste
- ☐ does research that has been applied in Singapore and China

2nd Listening   Complete the script by filling in the blanks.

Welcome to *Direct Talk*—interviews with leaders, visionaries, and pioneers who are shaping Asia and the rest of the world. Our guest today is Sun Xiaolong, a ¹( ) from Singapore. The world's population is growing, and managing the waste produced has become a ²( ) issue. Sun's research focuses on ³( ) heavy metals found in incineration ash and wastewater to make them non-toxic and recyclable. His goal is to achieve ⁴( ) toxic waste, and his research is already being ⁵( ) in Singapore and in China. We take a closer look at the ⁶( ) research and developments in what he does.

Checking Key Points

Watch Part 1 and choose the correct answers.

1. There are two types of garbage bins in Singapore, and the (blue / green) ones are used to collect non-recyclable garbage.

2. Singaporeans' awareness about (littering / separating trash) is not high enough.

3. In Singapore, waste is reduced to one-tenth of its original volume through (incineration / recycling).

4. In Singapore, there are (four / seven) incineration plants.

5. The incinerated ash is buried in a landfill (under high-rise buildings / on an uninhabited island).

Organizing Information

Explain Singapore's garbage disposal by completing the table.

City streets	In Singapore, there are strict laws against ¹( ).
Garbage disposal	**Recyclables** like glass, paper, plastics, and ²( ) are collected. **Non-recyclables** are burned in ³( ) plants.
Amount of waste generated	- 7.7 million tons of waste in 2018 - 1,500 tons of incinerated ⁴( ) per day
Incineration	**Process:** - Trash is burned at 700 to 1,000 degrees Celsius. - The remaining ash is taken to an offshore ⁵( ). **Problem:** This will ⁶( ) ( ) by 2035.

Interview

Part 2

[4:40]

online / video

Checking Key Points

Watch Part 2 and choose the correct answers.

1. Sun established (a waste management company / the Economic Development Board) in Singapore.

2. Toxic heavy metals (remain unchanged / become non-toxic) after incineration.

3. Sun developed reagents called ZA-TECH that (liquify / solidify) the metals.

4. These reagents are designed to work on (all heavy metals / one specific heavy metal).

5. Sun's technology is being used to treat (the soil at a landfill in Singapore / farmland in China).

Organizing Information

Explain the steps in the ZA-TECH method by completing the flowchart with items from the box below.

Problem	Heavy metals ¹( ) in the incinerated ash. Serious harm can be caused if they ²( ) the human body.

Step 1	**Step 2**	**Result**
³( ) reagents (ZA-TECH) into a solution containing heavy metals.	⁴( ) the solution.	The metals crystalize and ⁵( ). Once immobilized, they can be ⁶(**d**).

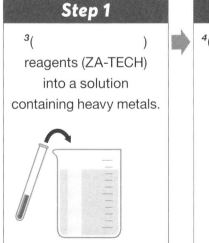  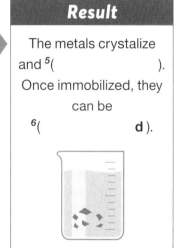

remove / enter / stir / solidify / accumulate / pour

The Words to Live By

art 2 3:59-4:40

  DL 49 CD 49

Confirm the conclusion of the interview by completing the script below.

Sun: As you can see from our company's name, my dream is a zero-waste world. "A calm mind

1 _____

_____." These are the words

of Zhuge Liang* to his son. Zhuge is **2** _____

_____ in *Romance*

*of the Three Kingdoms.*** Today, 1,700 years later, **3** _____

_____.

* Zhuge Liang 諸葛亮

** *Romance of the Three Kingdoms*『三国志演義』

Sharing Our Responses

1. Write down three new facts you learned from the interview. Share them with your partner.

2. With your partner, discuss and decide on a message for each of the following: Sun, residents of Singapore, and governments of the world. Share your messages with your classmates.

Taking the Next Step

In a group, find out how the following items are disposed of in your local areas/ hometowns and present your own ideas about how they could be better handled. Present your ideas to another group. Can you persuade them?

Items thrown away	How are they disposed of or recycled in your community?	How could they be better recycled or reused?
a Food		
b Fallen leaves		
c Computers		

Voice

13

Toru Oki

The Healing Power of Dogs

In this chapter, we'll learn about an activist's continuous efforts to introduce therapy dogs to Japan. Let's find out about some of the animal rights issues he is bringing to the public's attention.

Sharing Our Views

Think about the following questions and talk with your partner.

1. Do you have pets?
    Yes: What kinds? What are they like? How do they make you feel?
    No: Would you like a pet? Why or why not?

2. Have you heard of therapy dogs? What kinds of people do you think would benefit from having one?

3. What kinds of things do you think therapy dogs are trained to do?

Read this rehabilitation center pamphlet and answer the True/False questions below. The words in bold will appear in the interview.

Here to Stay: Animal-Assisted Therapy

A senior citizen suffering from **dementia** smiles for the first time in days when an **affectionate** cat is placed on her lap. A nine-year-old boy with cerebral palsy gradually builds **motor skills** by riding a pony every week. A teen who has been severely bullied regains self-esteem by **feeding** and interacting with a dog for 20 minutes each morning. These three people are benefiting from Animal-assisted Therapy (AAT), which takes advantage of the social bonds between humans and animals to treat a range of health concerns.

Although AAT was established as a new field in the 1990s, there has long been an understanding that animals have a therapeutic effect on us. Over 2,000 years ago, the "Father of Medicine," Hippocrates, wrote about horseback riding for people with serious illnesses. In early 19th-century England, patients at the York Retreat learned "behavioral management" by interacting with rabbits and chickens. In America, dog therapy was introduced for soldiers returning from WWI with mental health issues. During WWII, **rehabilitation** centers were opened for wounded or disabled veterans; part of their therapy was working **side by side** with farm animals and caring for dogs.

The last three decades have seen animal therapy programs started in hospitals, senior centers, schools, and even prisons. AAT is **acknowledged** as a **vital** part of many mental health programs, and several universities offer degrees in it. **Passionate advocates** for AAT highlight the **accomplishments** of individual therapy animals and the benefits to the animals themselves. It seems that AAT is here to stay.

1. A therapist might use AAT with both elderly patients and children.   T / F

2. The benefits of animals on humans were first recognized in the 1800s.   T / F

3. Students wishing to learn more about AAT can now major in it at school.   T / F

Boosting Vocabulary

(online / audio)   🎧 DL 51   ◉ CD 51

Match these words from the interview with their definitions.

1. stray   _____
2. give it a shot   _____
3. abandon   _____
4. purebred   _____
5. certified   _____
6. commendation   _____
7. euthanization   _____

a. award, honor
b. from only one breed
c. try, attempt
d. lost or homeless animal
e. leave behind, throw away
f. mercy killing
g. officially recognized

Introduction

Understanding the Main Topic   ▶ Part 1 0:00-00:47

(online / video)   (online / audio)   🎧 DL 52   ◉ CD 52

1st Listening   **Check ☑ the correct statements.**

Toru Oki _____.

- ☐ is a dog breeder
- ☐ introduced therapy dogs to Japan
- ☐ trains dogs to be champions for dog shows
- ☐ helps unwanted dogs

2nd Listening   **Complete the script by filling in the blanks.**

Welcome to *Direct Talk*—interviews with leaders, visionaries, and pioneers who are shaping Asia and the rest of the world. Our guest today is Toru Oki, a leading ¹(   ) for the use of therapy dogs. The animals provide comfort and ²(   ) to people who need it, including seniors and those ³(   ) from illness. Oki is said to be the person who ⁴(   ) introduced therapy dogs to Japan. And the dogs he trains are all ⁵(   ) or lost animals that would otherwise be put down. We asked Oki why he is such a ⁶(   ) champion of therapy dogs.

Checking Key Points

Watch Part 1 and choose the correct answers.

1. Oki has been involved with therapy dogs for over (30 / 40) years and now owns about (30 / 40) of them.

2. People with dementia can get their (energy / memory) back thanks to therapy dogs.

3. Therapy dogs can help the rehabilitation process by giving people a sense of (motivation / obligation).

4. Through training, dogs learn to (match the speed of / lead) the person they are walking with.

5. Completing the training curriculum takes therapy dogs (one and a half years / two and a half years).

Organizing Information

Describe therapy dogs and what they do by completing the table. The first letters are provided.

Kinds of dogs	Their training	How they help humans
- ^{1}(S) dogs - Abandoned dogs - Dogs who don't ^{2}(t) humans - Dogs picked up by animal services	**Time to master:** 2.5 years **Curriculum:** 50 different ^{3}(i) - Walking with someone using a ^{4}(c) - Matching speed to a person's	- Provide comfort and ^{5}(a) - Make them happy - Help improve their ^{6}(m) and motor skills

Interview **Part 2** [5:04]

online video

Checking Key Points

Watch Part 2 and choose the correct answers.

1. Oki (spent / borrowed) a lot of money to open a training school for therapy dogs.

2. At first, people in Japan (did not understand / embraced) the idea of therapy dogs.

3. In the U.S., most therapy dogs were (purebred / mixed-breed).

4. Oki (rescues / purchases) dogs from all over Japan and trains them to be therapy dogs.

5. Oki wants to (stop the forced euthanization of / establish hospitals for) unwanted animals.

Organizing Information

Retell the story of Oki and Chirori by completing the summary with items from the box below. Some of them are extra.

When Oki brought a therapy dog to Japan for the first time, he had to explain the idea to government ¹(   ), hospitals, and facilities. It was like fighting a ²(   ) for understanding. During that time, Oki rescued one ³(   ) dog named Chirori. Chirori did very well in training and became Japan's first ⁴(   ) therapy dog. She helped ⁵(   ) people during her life, helping them improve their motor skills, language skills, and more. People had no choice but to ⁶(   ) what a therapy dog can do.

acknowledge / battle / countless / certified
abandoned / purebred / awarded / officials

Confirm the conclusion of the interview by completing the script below.

Oki: My biggest desire is that ¹ _____ in Japan. It's simply not okay to have gas chambers where we're killing cats and dogs. I think ² _____. "All living things have the right to happiness." I've seen a lot of stray dogs in my day become amazing animals. These dogs can't be ³ _____ _____; that's something I feel very strongly about. And that's the idea behind these words.

" "

Sharing Our Responses

1. Write down three new facts you learned from the interview. Share them with your partner.

2. With your partner, discuss and decide on a message for each of the following: Toru Oki, Chirori, and a local government official in charge of animal euthanization. Share your messages with your classmates.

Taking the Next Step

The administration of the Wakabamura Hospital needs to know how therapy dogs could benefit their patients. With your group, create a poster persuading the staff to add therapy dogs to the treatments offered at the hospital. Refer to the p. 86 Organizing Information table and include:

1. Who the dogs are
2. How they have been trained
3. How they could help patients

Share your poster with your classmates. Can you persuade them to introduce a therapy dog program?

Voice

14

Mahzarin Banaji

Uncovering Our Hidden Biases

In this chapter, we'll learn about a Harvard professor's research into the gaps between what we think we believe and what we unconsciously believe. Let's find out how her experiments are done and what the results are.

Sharing Our Views

Think about the following questions and talk with your partner.

1. Are biases something we're born with or are they learned? Why do you think so?

2. Who is more biased, your parents' generation or yours? Why do you think so?

3. What positive biases (favorable images) do you think people have of the Japanese? Of women? Of scientists?

Read this blog entry and answer the True/False questions below. The words in bold will appear in the interview.

Lauryn's Blog

Biased? Me?

As a woman and as an African American, I know how bad **prejudice** feels. And until recently, I also thought I knew what kinds of people had **biases**. I even congratulated myself for being unbiased... until I joined an experiment in my psychology class two weeks ago.

Our professor explained that back in the 1950s, studies seemed to show that only certain types of people were biased. But now, researchers understand that our ideas about gender, race, and various social groups come from the culture around us; that's true for everyone, not just some people.

This happens early. By the time we're five years old, many biases are already **embedded** in our minds. At that young age, we don't have the ability to form our own opinions, so we accept biases that are **explicit** in mass media and **implicit** in the way society is structured.

Even when **well-intentioned** parents try to keep us unbiased, stereotypes are so easy—even comfortable—to believe. Part of the problem is **evolutionary**; we humans have always needed to feel like we belong to a group. And one way for us to feel good about our own group is to stereotype others: this group is dishonest, so we should be **suspicious** of them. That group is lazy because they have no **aspirations** for the future.

This needs to change. In the long term, I plan to **dedicate** myself to overcoming biases, including my own. **In the short term**, I'm going to take some more psychology classes!

1. At five years old, children are too young to begin forming biases. T / F

2. Negatively stereotyping others helps people feel good about themselves. T / F

3. The author's view of herself has changed since the beginning of her class. T / F

Boosting Vocabulary

online audio DL 55 CD 55

Match these words from the interview with their definitions.

1. impose _____
2. deviation _____
3. prescribe _____
4. excel _____
5. intervention _____
6. associate _____
7. attitude _____

a. getting involved to stop something
b. departing from the standard or norm
c. bring about by force
d. feeling toward someone or something
e. recommend as a medical treatment
f. be outstandingly good
g. link, connect

Introduction Understanding the Main Topic ▶ Part 1 0:00–0:52

online video online audio DL 56 CD 56

 **Check ☑ the correct statements.**

Mahzarin Banaji _____.

☐ teaches psychology
☐ focuses on gender issues in her research
☐ tries to explain prejudices
☐ claims that good people are religious

 **Complete the script by filling in the blanks.**

Welcome to *Direct Talk*—interviews with leaders, visionaries, and pioneers who are shaping Asia and the rest of the world. Today, we talk with the [1]( ) of Harvard University's Department of Psychology, Professor Mahzarin Banaji. Banaji has dedicated her [2]( ) to revealing the hidden prejudices which humans hold towards each other, whether it be gender, race, age, or [3]( ). Her book *Blindspot: Hidden Biases of Good People* explains how deeply this thought process is [4]( ) inside us. We ask Banaji about the costs this human behavior [5]( ) on society and how understanding them could [6]( ) the world we live in.

Interview Part 1 [3:52]

online / video

Checking Key Points

Watch Part 1 and choose the correct answers.

1. The main theme of Banaji's book is (how our mind works / how to change society).

2. Banaji gathers her data by (administering tests / distributing questionnaires) online.

3. The IAT asks participants to sort words into different categories and measures their (reaction times / intelligence levels).

4. The results of the Gender-Career IAT showed that a higher percentage of (men / women) strongly associate women with family.

5. Banaji says that IAT results can (reveal / deviate from) test-takers' explicit beliefs.

Organizing Information

Give an overview of the IAT and some of its results by completing the table.

What does IAT stand for?	Implicit ^{1}( ) Test
Where can we take the IAT?	Online
What does it try to determine?	^{2}( ) attitudes toward factors such as race or gender
How long does it take?	^{3}( ) minutes
What does it measure?	Participants' ^{4}( ) ( ) in sorting words
On the Gender-Career IAT, what percentages of participants associated women with family?	Male participants: ^{5}(-)% Female participants: ^{6}(-)%

Interview

[5:21]

online / video

Checking Key Points

Watch Part 2 and choose the correct answers.

1. Prescribing lower amounts of painkillers to some people illustrates an example of (race / gender) bias.

2. Research has shown that (Jane Smith / John Smith) is more likely to be given a job, even if Jane and John have the same qualifications.

3. Banaji believes that implicit bias actually (helps / hurts) our society.

4. The roots of implicit bias lie in our (evolutionary past / emotional attachments).

5. Anti-gay bias (increased / decreased) dramatically from 2008 to 2016.

Organizing Information

Describe Banaji's motivation for studying biases by completing the summary with items from the box below. Some of them are extra.

Implicit bias is considered partly responsible for the persistence of discrimination against ¹(   ) and women. Natural selection in human history is one thing that has made people ²(   ) of difference. However, today, ³(   ) with different people is essential to surviving in a global world. According to Banaji's findings, implicit bias can be reduced through ⁴(   ). She now hopes to discover why there are major ⁵(   ) in some biases while others do not seem to change.

---

ancestors / collaborating / gender bias / intervention
minorities / neutral / shifts / suspicious

🎧 DL 57 ◉ CD 57

Confirm the conclusion of the interview by completing the script below.

Narrator: We asked Mahzarin Banaji to write down some words which guide her. She writes, "Becoming civilized is to make the implicit explicit."

Banaji: As our world changes, a lot of the information that we carry implicitly in hidden ways that might actually ¹_____

_____ is no longer good for us, because our world is global. And so to me, part of becoming a civilized human is to try to ²_____

_____ of our minds, and to bring them into the light so we can observe them and say, "Is this still good for me? ³_____

_____?"

Sharing Our Responses

1. Write down three new facts you learned from the interview. Share them with your partner.
2. With your partner, discuss and decide on a message for each of the following: Professor Banaji, people with career biases, and doctors prescribing painkillers.

Taking the Next Step

IAT tests are available online and anyone can take them. If you're willing and interested in trying one:

1. Do an online search for the Implicit Association Test.
2. Try either the Gender-Career IAT or the Race IAT.
3. When you're finished, share your experience with a partner:
    - Was it difficult to complete the tasks?
    - What new vocabulary did you learn?
    - How did you feel about your own result?
    - How do you feel about contributing to this research?

Bill Nye

Space Exploration:
Can Private Citizens Play a Role?

In this chapter, we'll learn about a scientist's efforts to cultivate interest in science among private citizens. Let's also find out about some of the latest developments in space exploration.

Sharing Our Views

Think about the following questions and talk with your partner.

1. Did you enjoy studying science in elementary school? What about in junior and senior high school? Why or why not?

2. Do you believe in life on other planets? Why or why not?

3. Would you like to experience space exploration? Why or why not?

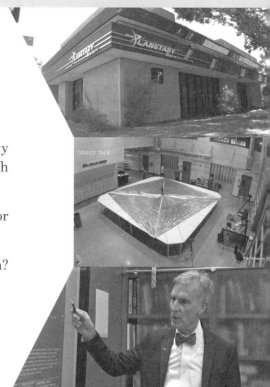

Read these presentation summaries from a science teachers' conference and answer the True/False questions below. The words in bold will appear in the interview.

10:00 – 10:55	Room 11-D
Inspiring the Astronomers of Tomorrow	Presenter: Yonggyu Lee

Fifty years ago, the first moon landing encouraged a generation of children to **pursue** careers in math, **mechanical engineering**, and science. However, a survey **conducted** earlier this year shows that today's kids would rather be athletes, musicians, or teachers than astronauts. This presentation will introduce several **campaigns** that are being **launched**, some by schools and others through **donations** from the **private sector**, to motivate elementary and junior high students to turn their attention to space.

11:00 – 11:25	Room 11-C
Searching for Life: An In-Class Debate	Presenter: Mira Kapoor

The idea of **living organisms** on **Mars, Venus**, or **Jupiter fascinates** some high school students; others are **convinced** that we are alone in **cosmic space**. It's the perfect topic for an in-class debate, but first, students must start learning the facts. The presenter will provide a reading list that will help students prepare to debate, as well as a series of lesson plans that will **further** students' understanding of the current search for life.

11:30 – 11:55	Room 12-A
Building Virtual Space Vessels	Presenter: Tomohito Nagami

For decades, engineers have designed rockets, satellites, and space stations with the aid of increasingly sophisticated software programs. With the *Cosmobuilder* game app, junior and senior high school students can design and launch their own space vessels into virtual reality, **soaring** above Earth's **surface** and avoiding **asteroids**! The presenter will demonstrate how *Cosmobuilder* helps students understand concepts like **propulsion** and gravity.

1. Becoming an astronaut is the top career goal for most children today.　　T / F
2. High school students already know a lot about life on other planets.　　T / F
3. Students can have fun and learn about science with the *Cosmobuilder*.　　T / F

Boosting Vocabulary

online / audio DL 59 CD 59

Match these words from the interview with their definitions.

1. vital _____
2. propel _____
3. deploy _____
4. orbit _____
5. verify _____
6. compelling _____
7. bureaucracy ____

a. move into position

b. cause to move forward

c. management system with levels of authority and fixed procedures

d. path of a celestial body or satellite

e. extremely important, essential

f. prove something exists or is true

g. convincing, very persuasive

Introduction

Understanding the Main Topic ▶ Part 1 0:00–0:57

online / video   online / audio  DL 60   CD 60

 1st Listening   Check ☑ the correct statements.

☐ The first human walked on the moon in 1969.
☐ The Planetary Society is part of NASA.
☐ Bill Nye is an astronomer.
☐ Bill Nye hosted a children's show.

2nd Listening   Complete the script by filling in the blanks.

Welcome to *Direct Talk*—interviews with leaders, visionaries, and pioneers who are shaping Asia and the rest of the world. In July 1969, the first human walked on the [1]( ) as part of NASA's historic Apollo 11 mission. Fifty years since then, [2]( ) sectors have become actively involved in space exploration. The Planetary Society is the world's largest [3]( ) space organization. Since 2010, Bill Nye has [4]( ) as its CEO. Nye is known as "the Science Guy" who became popular as the [5]( ) of a children's science show. He believes that time has come for private citizens and organizations to play a vital role in space exploration and [6]( ) science.

Checking Key Points

Watch Part 1 and choose the correct answers.

1. One of the core missions of the Planetary Society is to (educate people about science / support astronomers).

2. LightSail is a small spacecraft that is fueled by (a small battery / solar energy).

3. Once in orbit, LightSail can run (indefinitely / in any direction).

4. The LightSail project is funded by (donations / government agencies).

5. The first launch of LightSail was to test whether (photons could be collected / the sails would unfold) successfully in space.

Organizing Information

Give an overview of the Planetary Society by completing the table. The first letters are provided.

Who founded the Planetary Society? When?	**Who:** American scientists, including [1](a) Carl Sagan **When:** 1980
What are its core missions?	• To educate private [2](c) about space science • To [3](c) for more government space research
What did they develop?	• They developed the [4](s) LightSail and LightSail 2. • These are very [5](l) and are powered by [6](s).

Interview

[4:29]

online/video

Checking Key Points

Watch Part 2 and choose the correct answers.

1. Research shows that a lifelong passion for science (starts before the age of 10 / can be nurtured at any age).

2. As "the Science Guy," Nye tried to make each segment (full of scientific information / short and funny) for children.

3. PlanetVac is a project that aims to (clean up space / collect soil from planets).

4. Nye wants to find out whether there is (other life in the universe / another planet for humans to live on).

5. Nye points out that (bureaucracy / independence) is one of NASA's disadvantages.

Organizing Information

Summarize Nye's career by completing the table with items from the box below.

	Bill Nye...
1	studied ¹( ) at Cornell University.
2	worked for ²( ).
3	hosted ³( ) on TV for six years. has advocated for the ⁴( ) of science ever since.
4	became the CEO of the Planetary Society.
5	launched LightSail.
6	conducted the PlanetVac project, hoping to search for ⁵( ).
7	says that everyone asks two questions: 1) Where did we come from? 2) Are we alone in the ⁶( )?

a science show / Boeing / living organisms / mechanical engineering
space agency / joyfulness / universe / vessels

🎧 DL 61 ◉ CD 61

Confirm the conclusion of the interview by completing the script below.

Narrator: Lastly, we asked Nye about the words he lives by.

Nye: "Science is the best idea humans have ever had." [1]_____

_____. It's changed the world. And so the Planetary Society—we advance space science, which is the science of everything that's not on Earth. It's fantastic. We know—we have learned that the rules of nature—natural laws—seem [2]_____

_____, but everywhere in the universe—all over the cosmos. That's amazing. That's—[3]_____.

Sharing Our Responses

1. Write down three new facts you learned from the interview. Share them with your partner.

2. With your partner, discuss and decide on a message for each of the following: Bill Nye, elementary school science teachers, and kids under 10. Share your messages with your classmates.

Taking the Next Step

1. As a group of science teachers, do an online search for science shows (or videos about science) you could share in your class.

2. Choose one video your group members found. Include:
   a. The title and the scientific topics covered
   b. The target class (year and subject)
   c. Attractive features of the show

Explain the video to your classmates. Can you persuade them to show the video to their students?

Credit

All the interviews in *Inspiring Voices* are originally taken from NHK *Direct Talk*. Every effort has been made to trace the copyright holders of material used in this book. The publisher apologizes for any omissions and will be pleased to make necessary arrangements when *Inspiring Voices* is reprinted. Information in the interviews is as of when the episodes were originally broadcast.

このテキストのメインページ
www.kinsei-do.co.jp/plusmedia/412

次のページの QR コードを読み取ると
直接ページにジャンプできます

オンライン映像配信サービス「plus⁺Media」について

本テキストの映像と音声は plus⁺Media ページ（www.kinsei-do.co.jp/plusmedia）から、ストリーミング再生でご利用いただけます。手順は以下に従ってください。

ログイン

- ●ご利用には、ログインが必要です。
  サイトのログインページ（www.kinsei-do.co.jp/plusmedia/login）へ行き、plus⁺Media パスワード（次のページのシールをはがしたあとに印字されている数字とアルファベット）を入力します。

- ●パスワードは各テキストにつき 1 つです。
  有効期限は、<u>はじめてログインした時点から 1 年間</u>になります。

ログインページ

[利用方法]

次のページにある QR コード、もしくは plus⁺Media トップページ（www.kinsei-do.co.jp/plusmedia）から該当するテキストを選んで、そのテキストのメインページにジャンプしてください。

plus+Media トップ　　　メインページ

メニューページ　　　再生画面

「Video」「Audio」をタッチすると、それぞれのメニューページにジャンプしますので、そこから該当する項目を選べば、ストリーミングが開始されます。

[推奨環境]

iOS (iPhone, iPad)	OS: iOS 6 〜 13 ブラウザ：標準ブラウザ	Android	OS: Android 4.x 〜 10.0 ブラウザ：標準ブラウザ、Chrome
PC	OS: Windows 7/8/8.1/10, MacOS X　ブラウザ：Internet Explorer 10/11, Microsoft Edge, Firefox 48以降, Chrome 53以降, Safari		

※最新の推奨環境についてはウェブサイトをご確認ください。
※上記の推奨環境を満たしている場合でも、機種によってはご利用いただけない場合もあります。また、推奨環境は技術動向等により変更される場合があります。予めご了承ください。

このシールをはがすと
plus+Media 利用のための
パスワードが
記載されています。
一度はがすと元に戻すことは
できませんのでご注意下さい。
◀ここからはがして下さい
4120 Inspiring Voices

plus+Media

本書には CD（別売）があります

Inspiring Voices
15 Interviews from NHK Direct Talk

NHK Direct Talk——世界を変える声を聞く

2021 年 1 月 20 日　初版第 1 刷発行
2024 年 2 月 20 日　初版第 5 刷発行

編著者　小林めぐみ
　　　　藤田玲子
　　　　Peter J. Collins

発行者　福岡正人
発行所　株式会社　金星堂
（〒 101-0051）東京都千代田区神田神保町 3-21
Tel. (03) 3263-3828（営業部）
　　(03) 3263-3997（編集部）
Fax (03) 3263-0716
https://www.kinsei-do.co.jp

編集担当　西田碧　　　　　　　　　Printed in Japan
印刷所・製本所／大日本印刷株式会社

ISBN978-4-7647-4120-1　C1082

NHK NEWSLINE

NHK WORLD-JAPAN's flagship hourly news program delivers the latest world news, business and weather, with a focus on Japan and the rest of Asia.

— Daily / broadcast on the hour —

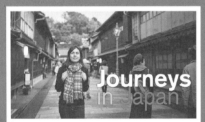

Journeys in Japan

Explore a different side of Japan. Meet the locals and discover traditions and cultures not usually found in guidebooks!

Tuesdays

Dining with the Chef

Traditional techniques and resourceful recipes! Chefs Saito and Rika, present their unique approaches to cooking delicious Japanese food.

Saturdays

GRAND SUMO Highlights

The best of today's sumo! Enjoy daily highlights of this dynamic sport with background info and play-by-play commentary adding to the excitement!

Daily (During tournaments)

NHK WORLD-JAPAN is the international service of NHK, Japan's public broadcaster. It offers a variety of English language programming on television and the internet

nhk.jp/world